JUNIOR Dictionary

First published in 2016 by Miles Kelly Publishing Ltd
Harding's Barn, Bardfield End Green, Thaxted, Essex, CM6 3PX, UK

2 4 6 8 10 9 7 5 3 1

Publishing Director Belinda Gallagher
Creative Director Jo Cowan
Editors Carly Blake, Rosie Neave, Sarah Parkin
Editorial Assistant Lauren White
Cover Designer Simon Lee
Designers Jo Cowan, Kayleigh Allen
Production Elizabeth Collins, Caroline Kelly
Reprographics Stephan Davis, Jennifer Cozens, Thom Allaway

ISBN 978-1-78617-342-3

Printed in China

British Library Cataloging-in-Publication Data
A catalog record for this book is available from the British Library

Made with paper from a sustainable forest

JUNIOR Dictionary

Author and consultant
Susan Purcell

How to use your dictionary

Cartoons

Look out for the fun cartoons that appear in each letter. How many different things can you see starting with the same letter?

Entries

*The words in **bold** are the entries, the words that you look up. There are more than 1,700 entries in your dictionary.*

Definitions

These come after each entry. They explain what the word means.

Example sentences

A sentence follows each definition. This gives you an example of the word within a sentence.

---

a b c d e f g h i j k l m n o p q r s **t** u v w x y z

How many things can you spot beginning with "t?"

Tt

table (tables)
1 a piece of furniture with legs and a flat top
Please clear the table.
2 a list of numbers or words written in rows and columns
We measured the height of everyone in the class and wrote the results in a table.

tadpole (tadpoles)
a very young frog or toad
Tadpoles have big heads and lo tails and live in water.

tail (tails)
the part of an animal at the of its back
The dog has a long, white tail.

tail

take (taking, took, t
1 to carry something
Take an umbrella with yo
2 to move something someone to another
Can you take us to th station?
3 to steal
The thieves took all the mone

Different forms of a word

Some entries are followed by the same word in plural form. This is when there is more than one of something. The plural is shown after the entry within brackets.

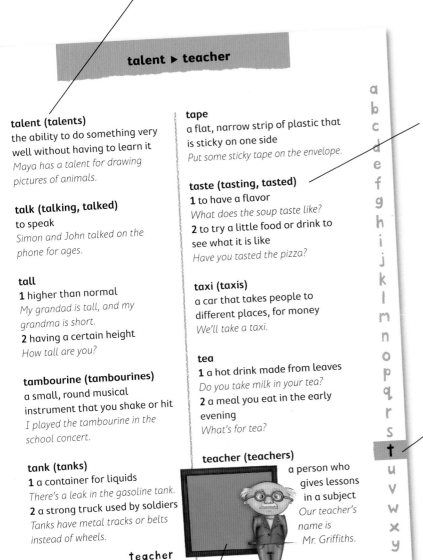

talent ▸ teacher

talent (talents)
the ability to do something very well without having to learn it
Maya has a talent for drawing pictures of animals.

talk (talking, talked)
to speak
Simon and John talked on the phone for ages.

tall
1 higher than normal
My grandad is tall, and my grandma is short.
2 having a certain height
How tall are you?

tambourine (tambourines)
a small, round musical instrument that you shake or hit
I played the tambourine in the school concert.

tank (tanks)
1 a container for liquids
There's a leak in the gasoline tank.
2 a strong truck used by soldiers
Tanks have metal tracks or belts instead of wheels.

tape
a flat, narrow strip of plastic that is sticky on one side
Put some sticky tape on the envelope.

taste (tasting, tasted)
1 to have a flavor
What does the soup taste like?
2 to try a little food or drink to see what it is like
Have you tasted the pizza?

taxi (taxis)
a car that takes people to different places, for money
We'll take a taxi.

tea
1 a hot drink made from leaves
Do you take milk in your tea?
2 a meal you eat in the early evening
What's for tea?

teacher (teachers)
a person who gives lessons in a subject
Our teacher's name is Mr. Griffiths.

teacher

a b c d e f g h i j k l m n o p q r s **t** u v w x y z

Verbs

If an entry is a verb (doing word) then other forms of the word will appear in brackets. For example, the verb "taste" is followed by different endings.

Alphabetical order

All of the entries are in alphabetical order. The alphabet is listed down the side of each page. Use the highlighted letters to help you find your way around.

Illustrations and photographs

These help you to understand the meaning of a word. Each illustration or photograph has its own label to tell you exactly what it is.

Puzzle time

These are fun things to do and give you a chance to play with words. This helps you to learn and remember them.

How many things can you spot beginning with "a?"

A a

above
1 in a higher place than something else
Annie lives in the room above.
2 more than
This ride is for children aged six and above.

absent
away from a place, not there
Sameer is absent today.

accident (accidents)
1 an unexpected event, often causing damage or injury
There was an accident on the road.
2 something that happens by chance
I dropped it by accident.

actor (actress; actors, actresses)
a person who plays a part in a movie or play
My Dad is an actor.

add

add (adding, added)
1 to put something together with something else
Add the milk and sugar to the butter.

2 to put numbers together to find the total
If you add twenty to fifteen it makes thirty-five.

address (addresses)
the house number and street where you live
My address is 65 Chestnut Avenue, Old Town.

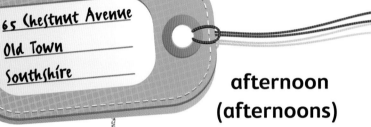

65 Chestnut Avenue
Old Town
Southshire

address

adult (adults)
a grown-up, not a child
Only adults are allowed in the pool after six p.m.

adult

adventure (adventures)
an exciting experience
Going on vacation with my friends is such a great adventure.

advert (advertisement; adverts, advertisements)
words or pictures in newspapers or on television about things for sale
There are too many advertisements in magazines.

afraid
scared, frightened
Are you afraid of snakes or spiders, or both?

afternoon (afternoons)
the part of the day between midday and the evening
We'll go out this afternoon.

again
another time, once more
Shall we sing it again?

age
the number of years someone has lived
At what age can I learn to drive?

air
the mixture of gases around us that we breathe
The air is clean and fresh.

aircraft (plural is the same)
machines that fly
Helicopters are a type of aircraft.

a
b
c
d
e
f
g
h
i
j
k
l
m
n
o
p
q
r
s
t
u
v
w
x
y
z

a

b c d e f g h i j k l m n o p q r s t

airplane (airplanes)
a large machine, with wings and an engine, that flies
Noisy airplanes fly over our house.

airport (airports)
a place where planes land and take off
The airport is very busy today.

alarm (alarms)
a machine that flashes or makes a noise as a warning
The burglar alarm is flashing!

alien (aliens)
something strange that comes from another planet
E.T. is a friendly alien.

alligator (alligators)
a type of large reptile that looks similar to a crocodile
Alligators spend much of their day in water, keeping cool and hidden from view.

alligator

alphabet (alphabets)
letters in a special order that form a language
"E" is a letter of the alphabet.

ambulance (ambulances)
a vehicle for taking people to and from hospital
Stop! There's an ambulance coming.

ambulance

anchor (anchors)
a heavy metal object on a rope or chain, which stops a boat moving.
Lower the anchor.

angel (angels)
a messenger from God, in some religions
In pictures, angels often have wings.

angry (angrier, angriest)
feeling or showing annoyance
My sister sometimes gets angry.

animal (animals)
a living thing that can move
Cows and horses are animals.

ankle (ankles)
the part of the body between the leg and the foot
I twisted my ankle when I fell over.

answer (answers)
1 something you say or write after a question
My answer is no.
2 the correct solution
Well done! That's the right answer.

answer (answering, answered)
1 to say or write something when asked a question
Where have you been? Please answer my question.
2 to pick up the telephone or go to the door
Please answer the telephone.

ant (ants)
a tiny insect that lives in groups
Some types of ant cut up leaves.

appear (appearing, appeared)
1 to look or to seem
She appears to be better today.
2 to come into sight
My sister appeared from behind me.

applause
clapping by a group of people to show they enjoyed something
Everyone gave a round of applause.

apple (apples)
a fruit that grows on trees
I always have an apple after lunch.

apple

apricot (apricots)
a small, fuzzy-skinned yellow fruit
I like dried apricots on cereal.

apron (aprons)
a piece of cloth that you put over your clothes to keep them clean
I wore an apron while I was painting.

arch

arch (arches)
a curved structure
We sat on the grass under the arch.

a b c d e f g h i j k l m n o p q r s t u v w x y z

a
b
c
d
e
f
g
h
i
j
k
l
m
n
o
p
q
r
s
t
u
v
w
x
y
z

arena (arenas)
a large building where you can
see sports events or concerts
I saw a football game in an arena.

argue (arguing, argued)
to strongly disagree
Let's not argue about the meal.

arm (arms)
the part of your body between
your shoulder and hand
Dad has broken his right arm.

**armchair
(armchairs)**
a chair that has
places for you to
rest your arms
*I like to read when
I'm sitting in an armchair.*

armchair

army (armies)
the people that fight for a
country on land
The Roman army was very powerful.

arrest (arresting, arrested)
to take someone to a police
station because they have
committed a crime
The police arrested the thief.

arrow (arrows)
a pointed stick that you shoot
from a bow
We fired arrows at the enemy.

art
the making of paintings,
drawings, and sculpture
My favorite subject at school is art.

artist (artists)
a person who makes art
He is a well-known artist.

ask (asking, asked)
1 to say something to someone
because you want them to tell
you something
"What is the time?" she asked.
2 to say you want something
I asked for a glass of water.

asleep
sleeping
*The baby is
fast asleep.*

asleep

assembly (assemblies)
a meeting of the whole school
We have an assembly every morning in the hall.

astronaut (astronauts)
a person who travels into space in a spacecraft
Astronauts walked on the Moon.

athlete (athletes)
a person who plays a sport
Athletes must train every day.

atlas (atlases)
a book with maps in it
I use an atlas at school.

attack (attacking, attacked)
to be violent and fight someone or something
Pirates attacked the ship.

attic (attics)
the inside of the roof of a house
There are some old books in the attic.

aunt (auntie; aunts, aunties)
the sister of your mother or father, the wife of your uncle
My aunt looks like my mother.

author (authors)
a person who writes books
Philippa Pearce is the author of Tom's Midnight Garden.

autograph (autographs)
the name of a famous person, written by them
May I have your autograph?

astronaut

automatic
if a machine is automatic it works by itself
The washing machine is automatic.

awake
not sleeping, not asleep
I tried to stay awake all night.

awful
very bad
This medicine tastes awful.

ax (axes)
a tool with a handle and a sharp cutting edge that is used for chopping wood
Dad chopped the tree down with an ax.

ax

a
b
c
d
e
f
g
h
i
j
k
l
m
n
o
p
q
r
s
t
u
v
w
x
y
z

a
b
c
d
e
f
g
h
i
j
k
l
m
n
o
p
q
r
s
t
u
v
w
x
y
z

How many things can you spot beginning with "b?"

B b

baboon (baboons)
a large monkey
Baboons are very noisy.

baby (babies)
a young child that has not yet learned to talk or walk
There is a new baby in the family.

baboon

babysitter (babysitters)
a person who looks after children while their parents are out
Our babysitter plays games with us.

back (backs)
1 the part of your body behind you, between your shoulders and bottom
I can swim on my back.
2 the part of something that is furthest from the front or from the way it is facing
The wires are at the back of the computer.

backward
the direction opposite to the way something is facing
Take four steps backward.

bacon
meat from a pig
We have bacon and eggs for breakfast.

bad (worse, worst)
not good or pleasant
It's bad news.

badge (badges)
something that you put on your clothes to show who you are or what you have done
I have four swimming badges.

badger (badgers)
an animal with black-and-white fur that lives underground
There is a family of badgers living in the woods.

badly
not done well
I play the piano badly.

badminton
a game that is played with rackets and a small object called a shuttlecock
We play badminton every day.

bag (bags)
a container made of plastic, paper, cloth, or leather
Let's put the vegetables into this bag.

baggy (baggier, baggiest)
loose, not tight
My sweater is too big and baggy.

bake (baking, baked)
to cook food in an oven
Bake the cake for 40 minutes.

balance
the ability to stay still without falling over
If I close my eyes I lose my balance.

balance (balancing, balanced)
1 to hold yourself still without falling over
Can you balance on this narrow bar?
2 to keep something steady without dropping it
The seal balanced a ball on its nose.

badminton

a
b
c
d
e
f
g
h
i
j
k
l
m
n
o
p
q
r
s
t
u
v
w
x
y
z

balcony (balconies)
an area outside a window where you can sit or stand
You can see the beach from the balcony.

bald
without hair
My dad is going bald.

bald

ball (balls)
a round object that you throw, hit, or kick in games
The ball went into the net.

ballet
a type of dancing that tells a story with no words
A very famous ballet is Swan Lake.

balloon (balloons)
a thin, rubber bag filled with air that is used as a decoration
We had balloons at the party.

banana (bananas)
a long, curved yellow fruit
I like bananas for breakfast.

balloons

band (bands)
1 a thin strip of material
Megan wears a band on her wrist.
2 a group of people who play music together
My brother plays the drums in a band.

bandage (bandages)
a piece of material that you wrap around an injury
The nurse put a bandage on Matthew's leg when he fell over.

bang (bangs)
a sudden loud noise
The door shut with a bang.

bank (banks)
1 a place to keep money
There is a bank in the town.
2 the land alongside a river
People sit on the bank and catch fish.

barbecue (barbecues)
a meal cooked over a flame outside
The weather's good. Let's have a barbecue.

bark

the hard material on a tree trunk

The bark is peeling off the tree in some places.

bark (barking, barked)

to make a short, loud noise, like a dog

My dog barks when someone knocks at the door.

barn (barns)

a farm building for keeping animals or crops

The cows are in the barn.

basket (baskets)

a container made of thin strips, to hold or carry things

Put the bread in the basket.

basketball

a game played by two teams that score points by throwing a ball through a round net

Basketball is a fast game.

bat (bats)

1 a small animal that usually flies at night

Bats have big ears and good hearing.

2 the wooden stick used to hit a ball in games such as baseball

I got a baseball bat for my birthday.

bathtub (bathtubs)

a long container that you fill with water and sit in to wash your body

In our bathroom there's a bathtub, washbasin, and toilet.

battery (batteries)

an object that makes electricity

My flashlight needs two batteries.

beach (beaches)

the area of land that is next to the sea

We played volleyball on the beach.

bean (beans)

the seed of a climbing plant that is eaten as food

I like baked beans on toast.

beans

a b c d e f g h i j k l m n o p q r s t u v w x y z

bear (bears)
a large, strong wild animal that is covered in fur
Bears sleep all winter.

beard (beards)
hair that grows on a man's chin and cheeks
My Dad has a beard.

beard

beautiful
lovely to look at
Roses are beautiful flowers.

bed (beds)
a piece of furniture for sleeping on
There are two beds in my room.

bedroom (bedrooms)
the room where you sleep
My bedroom is next to the bathroom.

bee (bees)
an insect with yellow-and-black stripes
Bees make honey.

beef
meat from a cow
We had roast beef and potatoes for dinner.

begin (beginning, began, begun)
to start
The story begins in the forest.

behind
at the back of someone or something
She's hiding behind the yard fence.

bell (bells)
a metal object that makes a ringing sound
The church bells ring every Sunday.

Puzzle time
Untangle the bees to see which one gets home

below
in a lower place than something else
The gym is on the floor below.

belt (belts)
a piece of clothing that you wear around your waist
My belt holds my pants up.

bench (benches)
a long seat for two or more people to sit on
I'll sit on the bench and wait for you.

bird

berry (berries)
a small, soft fruit that grows on bushes or trees
Blackberries and raspberries are types of berries.

better (best)
of a higher standard or quality
The new game is better than the last one.

between
in a place or time that separates two things or people
You can sit between us.

bicycle (bike; bicycles, bikes)
a machine with two wheels that you sit on and move by pushing on pedals
I'd like a new bicycle for my birthday.

bicycle

big (bigger, biggest)
1 large in size, not small
I need a big sports bag.
2 important
There's a big game on TV.

bill (bills)
a piece of paper money
Do you have a $10 bill?

bird (birds)
a creature that has wings, feathers, and lays eggs
There's a bird in the tree.

birthday (birthdays)
the day of the year on which a person is born
My birthday is September 25.

biscuit (biscuits)
a dry, thin cracker
My Mom likes biscuits and cheese.

bite (biting, bit, bitten)
to cut into something with your teeth
The dog bites!

a b c d e f g h i j k l m n o p q r s t u v w x y z

a b c d e f g h i j k l m n o p q r s t u v w x y z

bitter
having a strong, sharp taste such as coffee
Dark chocolate sometimes tastes very bitter.

blanket (blankets)
a piece of material on a bed that you use to keep warm
I'd like an extra blanket on my bed.

blind
not able to see
Some blind people carry white sticks.

blister (blisters)
a raised piece of skin, filled with liquid, caused by burning or rubbing
I have a blister on my foot.

blizzard (blizzards)
a very heavy snow storm
People shouldn't drive in a blizzard.

blood
red liquid that the heart pumps through your body
I cut my finger and now there's blood on my shirt.

blouse (blouses)
a shirt that girls and women wear
Our school blouse is blue and white.

blow (blowing, blew, blown)
to push air out of your mouth
It's fun to blow bubbles!

boat (boats)
a small ship
You get to the island by boat.

body (bodies)
1 the whole of a person
Skin covers your body.
2 a dead person
They covered the body with a sheet.

boat

bone (bones)
a hard, white part under the skin of a person or animal
Your skeleton has more than 200 bones.

bonfire (bonfires)
a fire outside
Dad made a bonfire in the yard.

book (books)
1 sheets of paper with writing on them, joined together for reading
This is a book about spiders.
2 sheets of paper joined together for writing on
Write your name on the cover of your school book.

books

boot (boots)
a strong shoe that covers your foot and ankle
You should wear your boots in the rain.

bored
not interested
I'm bored, let's play tennis or basketball outside.

boring
not interesting
This show is boring. Let's turn off the television.

born
starting life
My Dad was born in 1970.

borrow (borrowing, borrowed)
to take something that belongs to another person and give it back to them later
You can borrow the books for two weeks.

bottle (bottles)
a tall container for storing liquid
I have a water bottle on my bike.

bottom (bottoms)
1 the part of your body that you sit on
I fell on my bottom.
2 the lowest part of something
The number is at the bottom of the page.

bounce (bouncing, bounced)
to move back quickly after hitting or falling on something
The children bounced up and down on the trampoline.

bow (rhymes with low; bows)
1 a knot with loops
I tied my shoelaces in a bow.
2 a long, thin stick with string for shooting arrows or playing an instrument
You play the violin with a bow.

a b c d e f g h i j k l m n o p q r s t u v w x y z

bow (rhymes with cow; bowing, bowed)
to bend your body or your head to show respect
The servants all bowed to the king.

bowl (bowls)
a deep, curved dish
You eat cereal out of a bowl.

box (boxes)
a container with four sides
I keep my crayons in a box.

boxing
the sport of fighting with closed hands
My Dad likes watching boxing on TV.

boy (boys)
a male child or a young man
There are two boys in their family.

bracelet (bracelets)
a piece of jewelry worn around the wrist
My bracelet has my name on it.

boy

brain (brains)
the part of your body inside your head that you use for thinking, feeling, and moving
When you touch something hot, nerves send a message to your brain and you pull your hand away.

branch

branch (branches)
the part of a tree that grows out from the trunk
Leaves, flowers, and fruit grow on branches.

brave
not afraid to do dangerous things
Soldiers are very brave.

bread
a type of food made with flour, water, and yeast
I like jelly on bread.

break (breaking, broke, broken)
to make something separate into two or more pieces
I dropped the glass and broke it.

a b c d e f g h i j k l m n o p q r s t u v w x y z

breakfast (breakfasts)
the first meal of the day
We always have cereal for breakfast.

breath (breaths)
the air that goes in and out of your body
Take a deep breath and smell the fresh air.

breathe (breathing, breathed)
to take air into your body and let it out
Breathe in, and slowly breathe out.

breeze (breezes)
a light wind
There's a lovely warm breeze blowing.

brick (bricks)
a block of baked clay used for building
The wall is made with bricks.

bridge (bridges)
a structure built to join two things
There is a bridge over the river.

bright
1 full of light
It's a bright, sunny day.
2 strong and easy to see
Yellow and orange are bright colors.
3 clever, intelligent
That's a bright idea.

brilliant
1 very bright and strong
There was a brilliant light in the sky.
2 very good at doing something
She's a brilliant scientist.
3 very good or enjoyable
This is a brilliant book, you should read it.

bring (bringing, brought)
to take something with you
Don't forget to bring a jacket with you. It's cold!

broccoli
a green vegetable that looks like a little tree
Let's have broccoli with our dinner.

bridge

a b c d e f g h i j k l m n o p q r s t u v w x y z

a
b
c
d
e
f
g
h
i
j
k
l
m
n
o
p
q
r
s
t
u
v
w
x
y
z

broom (brooms)
a brush with a handle
Sweep the floor with a broom.

brother (brothers)
a boy or a man who has the same
parents as another person
Nadia has two brothers.

bruise (bruises)
a blue or purple mark on the skin
that appears after something has
hit you
I've got a big bruise on my arm.

brush (brushes)
a tool that has stiff hairs fastened
to a handle that is used for
sweeping, painting, or cleaning
*When you've
finished
painting, put
the brush in the
jar of water.*

**bubble
(bubbles)**
a small ball of
air in a liquid
*Soda has got lots
of little bubbles
in it.*

bucket (buckets)
a round, open container with a
handle
The bucket was full of water.

**budgie
(budgerigar;
budgies,
budgerigars)**
a small, brightly
colored bird that
some people keep
as a pet
Our budgie lives in a cage.

budgie

build (building, built)
to make something, such as a
house, by putting pieces together
*There are plans to build a new
school next year.*

building (buildings)
a place with a roof and
walls
*Houses, stores, and
schools are all buildings.*

bull (bulls)
a male cow, elephant,
or whale
*We saw a bull with a
ring in his nose.*

Puzzle time
Which of these brushes
is the odd one out?

answer:
broom, it
doesn't end
in "brush".

bunch (bunches)
a group of things that are attached together
There's a bunch of grapes on the table.

bunch

burger (burgers)
a flat cake of meat or vegetables
We each had a burger and fries for dinner.

burglar (burglars)
a person who goes into buildings to steal things
A burglar stole the money.

burn (burning, burnt, burned)
1 to be on fire
The candles are burning.
2 to destroy something with fire
We burned all the trash on a bonfire.

bus (buses)
a vehicle that carries passengers
I get the bus to school.

bush (bushes)
a small tree with lots of branches
Berries grow on bushes.

busy (busier, busiest)
1 doing things, working hard
Mom's busy on the computer.
2 lively, full of people
The town center is always very busy on a Saturday.

butcher (butchers)
a person who cuts up and sells meat
Our butcher always wears a striped apron.

butter
yellow food that is made from milk
Use a knife to spread butter on the bread.

butterfly (butterflies)
an insect with large wings
Butterflies drink from flowers.

button (buttons)
a round object that fastens clothes
My shirt has six buttons.

buy (buying, bought)
to get something by paying money for it
Shall we buy some candy?

a
b
c
d
e
f
g
h
i
j
k
l
m
n
o
p
q
r
s
t
u
v
w
x
y
z

abcdefghijklmnopqrstuvwxyz

How many things can you spot beginning with "c?"

Cc

cabbage (cabbages)
a large vegetable with thick, round leaves
Rabbits love eating cabbages.

cabin (cabins)
1 a small house made of wood, usually in the country
The cabin is halfway up the mountain.

2 the place where the passengers sit inside an airplane
The pilot walked back through the cabin.

3 a small room to sleep in on a ship
The cabin has two beds.

cactus (cacti or cactuses)
a plant that grows in hot, dry places, and that has needles instead of leaves
Cacti don't need much water.

café (cafés)
a place that serves drinks and simple meals
Why don't we stop and have lunch at a café?

cabbage

cage (cages)
a room or box with bars in which to keep animals or birds
Pet hamsters and mice live in cages.

cake (cakes)
a sweet food made of flour, sugar, and eggs that is baked in an oven
Mom baked a chocolate cake.

calculator (calculators)
a machine that adds up numbers and does other sums
I use a calculator in math lessons.

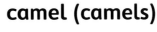

calendar (calendars)
a chart that shows the days, weeks, and months of the year
We wrote everyone's birthday on the calendar.

calf (calves)
1 a baby cow, elephant, or whale
The calf is two days old.
2 the back part of your leg between your ankle and knee
I've pulled a muscle in my calf.

call (calling, called)
1 to shout or say something in a loud voice
Dad called out to us.
2 to telephone
I'll call you when I get home.
3 to visit
The doctor calls when someone is very ill.
4 to give someone or something a name
They called the baby Luke.

camel (camels)
a large animal with one or two humps that can carry heavy loads
A camel can go without water for a long time.

camel

camera (cameras)
a piece of equipment used for taking photographs or filming
The teacher brought her camera on the school trip.

camp (camps)
a place where people stay in tents
The camp is over the hill.

a b **c** d e f g h i j k l m n o p q r s t u v w x y z

camp (camping, camped)
to stay in a tent
Every summer, we camp in the yard.

can (cans)
a metal container
We collect soda cans for charity.

can (could)
1 to be able to do something
Aziz can play the violin.
2 to be allowed to do something
We can come to your party.

candle (candles)
a stick of wax with a string through it that you burn for light
Let's light the candles on the cake.

candles

candy (candies)
a small piece of sweet, sugary food such as a chocolate or toffee
Clean your teeth after eating candy.

canoe (canoes)
a small boat that is pointed at both ends
You use a paddle to make a canoe move through the water.

capital (capitals)
the main town in a country
Do you know which city is the capital of France?

capital letter (capital letters)
a large letter of the alphabet
THIS SENTENCE IS WRITTEN IN CAPITAL LETTERS.

captain (captains)
1 someone who leads a team
Who is captain of the basketball team this year?
2 a person who is in charge of a ship or a plane
The captain has told us that the flight will take two hours.

car

car (cars)
a machine on wheels that has an engine and that people can ride in
I have bought a new car. It is bright orange.

card (cards)
1 thick, stiff paper (no plural)
We stuck the pictures onto card.
2 a piece of card with words and a picture that you give or send someone
My brother gave me a birthday card.
3 a piece of stiff paper or plastic that you use to buy things or to identify yourself
I have a library card.
4 a piece of stiff paper with pictures and numbers that you use to play games
Each player has seven cards.

cards

cardigan (cardigans)
a piece of clothing like a sweater with buttons down the front
Wear a cardigan if it's cold.

careful
paying attention to what you are doing so that you don't make a mistake or have an accident
Be careful! That knife is sharp.

carnival (carnivals)
an outdoor show with rides and games
We all go to the carnival every year.

carol (carols)
a religious Christmas song
My favorite carol is O Little Town of Bethlehem.

carpet (carpets)
a thick cover for the floor
The carpet in my bedroom is blue and green.

carrot (carrots)
a long, orange vegetable that grows under the ground
Carrots are a healthy food to eat.

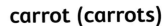
carrots

carry (carrying, carried)
to move something from one place to another
Can you help me carry these bags please?

cartoon (cartoons)

1 a funny drawing in a newspaper or comic

There is a cartoon every day in most newspapers.

2 a movie with animation instead of real actors

I like watching cartoons on television.

castle (castles)

a large, strong building with thick walls

Sleeping Beauty lived in a castle.

cat (cats)

a small, furry animal with a long tail and sharp claws

My cat likes to climb trees.

cat

catch (catching, caught)

1 to get hold of something when someone throws it

I'll throw the ball and you can try to catch it.

2 to get an illness

People often catch a cold in winter.

3 to get on a bus, train, or plane and go somewhere

We usually catch the bus to school.

castle

caterpillar (caterpillars)

an animal, like a worm with legs, that turns into a butterfly or a moth

Caterpillars eat leaves.

cave (caves)

a hole in a mountainside or under the ground

Caves are usually dark and damp.

CD (compact disc; CDs, compact discs)

a circular piece of plastic for storing sound

Have you bought their latest CD? It's really good!

celery

a long, green, crunchy vegetable

Mom chopped up some celery.

cell phone (cell phones)
a small telephone that people carry around
Call me on my cell phone.

cellar (cellars)
a room underneath a house or other building
We keep our bikes in the cellar.

cereal
a breakfast food that is made from wheat, oats, or rice
I always put sugar on my cereal.

chair (chairs)
a piece of furniture for sitting on
Pull your chair close to the desk.

chalk
a soft, white rock
I drew a picture using chalk.

chameleon (chameleons)
a lizard that changes color so its skin matches the things around it
A chameleon catches its prey using its long, sticky tongue.

chameleon

change (changing, changed)
1 to become different or to make something different
You haven't changed at all!
2 to put on different clothes
I'm cold—I'll change my top.

cheap
not expensive
My watch was cheap. I bought it in the sale.

cheese
a food that is made from milk
I'd like more cheese on my pizza.

cheese

cheetah (cheetahs)
a wild animal of the cat family with black spots
Cheetahs can run very fast.

cherry (cherries)
a small, round, reddish fruit with a pit in the center
We had cherries and ice cream for dessert.

chess
a board game for two people
Chess is my favorite game.

a b c d e f g h i j k l m n o p q r s t u v w x y z

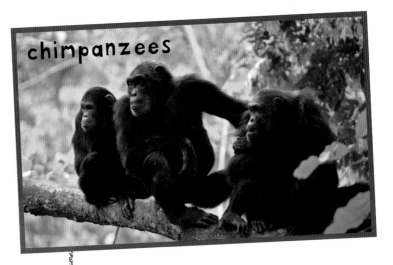
chimpanzees

chest (chests)
1 the part of your body between your neck and your stomach
Men have hair on their chests.
2 a strong box with a top that locks
The pirates hid the gold in a chest.

chestnut (chestnuts)
a big, brown, shiny nut that grows on trees
We had roasted chestnuts at the party.

chicken (chickens)
a farm bird kept for its eggs and meat, or the meat from this bird
A female chicken is called a hen.

child (children)
1 a young person
Every child has to go to school
2 someone's son or daughter
My eldest sister has just one child.

chimney (chimneys)
an opening over a fire that takes smoke out through the roof of a building
Smoke was coming from the chimney.

chimpanzee (chimp; chimpanzees, chimps)
a small ape with fur and no tail
I saw chimpanzees at the zoo.

chin (chins)
the part of your face under your mouth
His beard hides his chin.

chips
thin pieces of potato that have been cooked until crisp
Which flavor chips would you like?

chocolate
a sweet food made from cocoa beans
Would you like a piece of chocolate?

chocolate

choir (choirs)
a group of singers
I sing in the school choir.

Christmas
a Christian holiday in December
I got lots of great presents for Christmas.

church (churches)
the place where Christians meet to worship
My uncle got married in a church.

circus (circuses)
a show with people and animals, held in a big tent
The circus is in town! Are you coming?

city (cities)
a large town
New York is an exciting city.

claws

clap (clapping, clapped)
to make a loud sound by hitting the palms of your hands together
We clapped until our hands hurt at the end of the show.

class (classes)
1 a group of people who learn together
We're in the same math class at school.

2 a group of things or animals that are similar
People belong to the class of animals called mammals.

classroom (classrooms)
a room in a school where you have lessons
Our classroom is next to the hall.

claw (claws)
a sharp, hard nail on an animal's foot
My cat scratched me with her claws.

clean
not dirty
The car is clean and shiny.

clean (cleaning, cleaned)
to make something tidy, to take dirt away
Mom told me to clean my room because it was very untidy.

clear
1 easy to understand, hear, or read
The instructions are clear.
2 easy to see through
You can see the fish swimming in the clear water.

a b **c** d e f g h i j k l m n o p q r s t u v w x y z

clever
able to learn or understand things quickly or well
Well done. You're very clever.

cliff (cliffs)
a rock or mountain next to the ocean
The road runs along a cliff.

climb (climbing, climbed)
to move upward
She climbed to the top of the ladder.

clock (clocks)
a machine that tells the time
The clock said 5:55 a.m.

close (rhymes with dose)
near
The hotel is close to the beach.

clock

close (closing, closed) (rhymes with rose)
to shut
The store closes at six o'clock.

closet (closets)
a cupboard to hang clothes in
I have a closet in my bedroom.

cloth (cloths)
1 a soft material
The chair is covered in cloth.
2 a piece of cloth for a special purpose
Clean the window with a cloth.

clothes
things that people wear
I've grown and now my clothes don't fit me.

cloud (clouds)
a white or gray object in the sky that is made of tiny drops of water
There are a few clouds in the sky.

clown (clowns)
someone who makes people laugh
There was a clown at Tom's party.

coach (coaches)
1 a large bus
We went to the zoo by coach.
2 a person who trains people in sport
The baseball team is looking for a new coach.

coast
the land next to the sea
The town is on the coast.

coat (coats)
a piece of clothing you wear over your clothes to stay warm
I hang up my coat when I get to school.

cobweb (cobwebs)
a thin net that a spider spins to catch insects
There are cobwebs in the cellar.

cobweb

coconut (coconuts)
the nut of the palm tree
Coconuts have a white juice inside them.

cocoon (cocoons)
the bag around an insect that protects it while it is growing into an adult
The cocoon broke open and a butterfly flew out.

coffee
a hot drink made from the brown beans of a plant
Do you take sugar in your coffee?

coin (coins)
a piece of money that is made of metal
They keep coins from their vacations.

cold
not warm or hot
Brrr—this water is very cold.

collect (collecting, collected)
to put things together in one place
Some people collect coins.

color (colors)
blue, green, red, or yellow
What color is your jacket?

color (coloring, colored)
to make something a color, for example with paint or crayons
We colored in the picture.

comb (combs)
an object for making your hair tidy
Don't let anyone use your comb.

comb

comic (comics)
a magazine with pictures that tell a story
The story in this comic is very funny.

a b c d e f g h i j k l m n o p q r s t u v w x y z

compass (compasses)

an object that shows you what direction you are traveling in

Read the compass to find the treasure!

competition (competitions)

a test to see who is best at something

There was a singing competition on the radio.

complain (complaining, complained)

to say that something is wrong and that you are unhappy with it

He complained to the waiter.

computer (computers)

a machine for storing information and doing jobs such as writing letters

You can play games on computers.

concentrate (concentrating, concentrated)

to pay attention to what you are doing

I can't concentrate on my work because it's so noisy.

concert (concerts)

a show where people play music

I'm playing the violin in the concert.

confused

a feeling of not being sure

I was confused by the question.

container (containers)

something that holds something else in it

Jars, cans, and boxes are containers.

continent (continents)

one of the seven large areas of land in the world

Africa, North America, and Europe are all continents.

cook (cooks)

a person who prepares food

The cook has to make meals for 200 children every day.

cook (cooking, cooked)

to make food hot so it can be eaten

Ahmed is cooking dinner for us.

cook

cool
a little bit cold
There is a cool breeze.

copy (copying, copied)
to do something the same as something else
The teacher writes a sentence and we copy it.

corn
the seeds of the maize plant, or the plant itself
Popcorn and cornflakes are made from corn.

cottage

cottage (cottages)
a small house, usually in the country
My granny lives in a little cottage.

cough (coughing, coughed)
to force air from your throat
She's still coughing. Give her a drink of water.

count (counting, counted)
to find out how many
The teacher counted the books.

country (countries)
1 a place with its own government
France and Italy are European countries.
2 land away from cities and towns
We live in a house in the country.

cousin (cousins)
the child of your aunt or uncle
Charlie is my cousin.

cow (cows, cattle)
a large, female farm animal that gives milk
Cows eat grass.

cowboy (cowboys)
a man who rides a horse and takes care of cattle
The cowboy is wearing a big hat and boots.

crab

crab (crabs)
a sea creature that moves sideways and has big claws
I saw a crab in a pool on the beach.

a b c d e f g h i j k l m n o p q r s t u v w x y z

crack (cracks)
a line where something
is broken
There's a crack in this mug.

**crack (cracking,
cracked)**
to break something so
that a line appears on it
I've cracked your plate. Sorry!

crane (cranes)
a large machine that lifts very
heavy things
*The crane lifted the huge box and
put it on the ship.*

crash (crashes)
1 an accident when two or more
things bump into each other
My uncle had a crash in his car.
2 a loud noise
The loud crash hurt my ears.

crash (crashing, crashed)
1 to have an accident by
bumping into something
The car crashed into a tree.
2 to suddenly stop
working
*The computer has crashed and
now I've lost all my work.*

cracks

**crawl (crawling,
crawled)**
to move around
on your hands
and knees
*The baby is
starting to crawl.*

crayon (crayons)
a small pencil made from colored
wax
*Use your crayons to finish the
picture.*

cream
the thick, yellowish-white liquid
at the top of milk
*I love strawberries and cream in
summer.*

creature (creatures)
any animal
The blue whale is a huge creature.

crash

a b c d e f g h i j k l m n o p q r s t u v w x y z

creep (creeping, crept)
to move so that no one sees or hears you
We crept quietly through the bushes in the park.

cricket
1 a game played by two teams. The aim is to hit the ball and score runs
At school, we play baseball in winter and cricket in summer.
2 (crickets) an insect that makes a noise by rubbing its wings together
I've seen crickets in the yard. They live under rocks and logs.

crocodile

crocodile (crocodiles)
a large animal with a long body, short legs, and big teeth
Crocodiles like floating in the water.

crooked
not straight
The fence is very crooked.

crop (crops)
plants that are grown for people and animals to eat, or that are used to make things
The weather is very important to farmers who grow crops.

cross (crosses)
two lines that go over each other like the letter x
There is a cross on the map where the treasure is hidden.

cross (crossing, crossed)
to go from one side of something to the other
We looked both ways then crossed the road.

crowd (crowds)
a lot of people in one place
There was a big crowd of people outside the store.

crown

crown (crowns)
a metal circle that kings and queens wear on their heads
The king is wearing a gold crown.

cruel (crueller, cruellest)
not kind
We must not be cruel to animals.

crumb (crumbs)
a small piece of something such
as bread or cake
*Who's eaten the cake? There are
only a few crumbs left.*

cry (crying, cried)
1 to have tears coming from your
eyes, usually because you feel
sad or are hurt
*The little boy
cried when
he fell over.*
2 to shout
*"Help! Help!"
they cried.*

crying

cucumber (cucumbers)
a long, thin green vegetable that
you put in salads
Cucumbers contain a lot of water.

cuddle (cuddling, cuddled)
to hold someone in your arms to
show you care
*Chloe cuddled her friend to cheer
her up.*

cup (cups)
a container with a handle for
drinking from
I'd like a cup of hot milk please.

cupboard (cupboards)
a piece of furniture for storing
things
*Please dry the dishes and put them
in the cupboard.*

curious
wanting to know or find
out about something
Cats are very curious.

curls

curl (curls)
a piece of hair that
is curved at the end
She has beautiful curls.

curtain (curtains)
cloth that hangs across
or over a window
We close the curtains at night.

cushion (cushions)
a bag with soft material inside for
sitting or lying on
*This chair is hard. I'm going to put a
cushion on it.*

cut (cutting, cut)
to use a knife or scissors to break
something or make it smaller
*We all sang "Happy Birthday," then
she cut the cake.*

How many things can you spot beginning with "d?"

Dd

daffodil (daffodils)
a yellow flower
that comes out
in spring
*I bought my mom a
bunch of daffodils.*

daffodils

daisy (daisies)
a flower with white
petals and a yellow center
*Sophie picked some daisies to make
a daisy chain.*

damage (damaging, damaged)
to spoil or break something
*A big dog damaged the fence at the
bottom of the yard.*

dance (dancing, danced)
to move your body to music
Let's dance to this music.

**dandelion
(dandelions)**
a wild flower with
thin, yellow petals
and fluffy seeds
*There are dandelions
growing on the lawn.*

dangerous
not safe
Playing with matches is dangerous.

a b c **d** e f g h i j k l m n o p q r s t u v w x y z

a b c **d** e f g h i j k l m n o p q r s t u v w x y z

dark
not light
It's too dark to play outside.

date (dates)
1 the number of a day in a month
What's the date today?
2 a sweet fruit from a palm tree
Dates are sticky and chewy.

daughter (daughters)
a female child
Mr. and Mrs. Patel have two daughters.

day (days)
1 a 24-hour period
We're staying here for three days.
2 the time between the early morning when the sun rises and the time it sets
Bats do not fly during the day.

dead
not alive
This plant looks dead. Did you water it?

deaf
not able to hear
Many deaf people can read lips.

dear
1 a word to start a letter
Dear Mr. and Mrs. Anderson, How are you?
2 much loved
I've known Claire for years. She's a very dear friend.

deep
a long way from the top to the bottom
I'm not afraid to swim in the deep end of the pool.

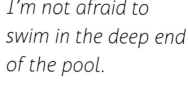

deer

deer
an animal that lives in forests
Deer are gentle animals.

delicious
tasting very good
This ice cream is delicious.

delighted
very happy
I'm delighted with my new bike.

den (dens)
1 a wild animal's home
The fox went back to its den.
2 a room used for reading and watching television
Shall we watch a movie in the den tonight?

dentist (dentists)
a person who looks after people's teeth
I go to the dentist every six months.

desert (deserts)
a place where there is very little or no rain
Camels live in the desert.

desk (desks)
a piece of furniture that you sit at to read, write, or use a computer
There's a lamp on my desk.

dessert (desserts)
sweet food that you eat at the end of a meal
What's for dessert? Is it ice cream?

dessert

detective (detectives)
a person who follows clues to find out about a crime and who did it
The detective asked me questions.

diamond (diamonds)
a very hard, clear stone that is used to make jewelry
Diamonds are very expensive.

diary (diaries)
a book with the days of the year in it where you write what you plan to do, or what you have done
I write the birthdays of my friends and family in my diary.

dice

die (dice)
a cube with spots on each side that is used for playing games
It's your turn—throw the dice.

die (dying, died)
to stop living
Water the plant before it dies.

a b c **d** e f g h i j k l m n o p q r s t u v w x y z

a b c d e f g h i j k l m n o p q r s t u v w x y z

different
not the same
The two sisters are very different.

difficult
not easy
I hope the spelling test isn't too difficult.

dig (digging, dug)
to make a hole in the ground
Let's dig a hole in the sand.

digital
1 showing information using numbers that can change
This is a digital watch.
2 storing information using a special computer code
My mom uses a digital camera.

dining room (dining rooms)
the room in which you eat your meals
The dining room is next to the kitchen in our house.

dinner (dinners)
the main evening meal
We're having lasagna and salad for dinner.

dinner

dinosaur (dinosaurs)
an animal that became extinct millions of years ago
We learned all about dinosaurs at the history museum.

dinosaur

dirty (dirtier, dirtiest)
not clean
Please take off your dirty shoes before you come in.

disabled
a disabled person cannot use part of their body
This parking space is for disabled drivers only.

disappear (disappearing, disappeared)
to go out of sight or become impossible to find
The sun disappeared behind a cloud.

disco (discos)
a place or a party where people dance
There's a disco on Saturday.

discover (discovering, discovered)
to find something for the first time
The farmer discovered some old coins in his field.

disease (diseases)
an illness
Injections stop you from getting some diseases.

disguise (disguises)
something that you wear to hide who you really are
He came to the party in disguise.

dive

dish (dishes)
a bowl or plate, used for serving food
Please dry the dishes.

disk (disks)
a thin, round piece of plastic for storing computer information
Save the file on a disk.

district (districts)
an area of a town or country
Emily and I live in the same district.

disturb (disturbing, disturbed)
to speak to someone when they are doing something
Please don't disturb James while he's doing his homework.

ditch (ditches)
a long, narrow hole in the ground along the side of a road or field
Don't fall into the ditch!

dive (diving, dived)
to go into water headfirst
I can dive to the bottom of the pool.

divide (dividing, divided)
to separate or share something
Let's divide the pizza between us.

dizzy (dizzier, dizziest)
feeling that things are turning around you or that you are going to fall
That ride makes me dizzy.

doctor (doctors)
a person who looks after sick people
My uncle is a doctor. He works at the hospital.

a b c **d** e f g h i j k l m n o p q r s t u v w x y z

document (documents)

1 a set of papers that contain official information
We keep important documents in this cupboard.

2 a piece of work that is saved in a file on a computer
You can attach a document to an e-mail.

dog (dogs)
an animal that people keep as a pet
Our dog is called Prince.

dog

doll (dolls)
a toy in the shape of a person
Let's play with our dolls.

dolphin (dolphins)
a large, warm-blooded creature that lives in the ocean
A dolphin looks like a fish but it is an air-breathing mammal.

domino (dominoes)
a piece of black wood or plastic with white spots that is used to play games
Each person has five dominoes.

donkey (donkeys)
an animal that looks like a small horse with long ears
Every day we feed carrots to the donkey in the field near our house.

donut (donuts)
a small, round, sugary cake that has been fried in hot oil
Some donuts have a hole in the middle.

door (doors)
something that you open and close to go into or out of a room, house, or car
It's cold, shall we shut the door?

dolphins

down
toward a lower place
Get down off the ladder.

download (downloading, downloaded)
to put information from the Internet onto your computer or other electronic device
I downloaded the song to my iPod.

dragon

dragon (dragons)
an imaginary animal like a big lizard that breathes fire
The story is about a beautiful princess trapped in a big, red dragon's cave.

dramatic
very exciting with lots of action
The show had a very dramatic ending.

draw (drawing, drew, drawn)
to make a picture
I can't draw people very well. I'm better at drawing animals.

drawer (drawers)
part of a piece of furniture that slides in and out that is used for storing things
Put the socks in the drawer.

dream (dreams)
a story that happens in your mind when you are asleep
I had a bad dream last night.

dream (dreaming, dreamt, dreamed)
1 to see things in your sleep
I dreamt that I could fly.
2 to hope for something
We dream of winning the Super Bowl.

dress (dresses)
a piece of clothing for girls or women that has a top and skirt
I'm wearing a dress for the party.

dress

dress (dressing, dressed)
to put clothes on yourself or someone else
My mom dresses us alike because we're twins.

a b c **d** e f g h i j k l m n o p q r s t u v w x y z

a
b
c
d
e
f
g
h
i
j
k
l
m
n
o
p
q
r
s
t
u
v
w
x
y
z

drink (drinks)
liquid that you take in your mouth and swallow
I'm thirsty. Can I have a drink please?

drink (drinking, drank, drunk)
to take liquid into your mouth and swallow it
I drank a whole glass of orange juice.

drive (driving, drove, driven)
to control a vehicle, such as a car
Our mom drives us to and from school every day.

drop (dropping, dropped)
to fall or to let something fall
Please don't drop that vase. It was very expensive.

drum (drums)
a musical instrument that you hit with a stick or your hand
My brother got a set of drums for his birthday. When he plays, he makes a lot of noise!

dry (drier, driest or dryer, dryest)
not wet
The washing is dry. Please can you put it away?

ducks

duck (ducks)
a bird with webbed feet that lives near water
We feed bread to the ducks at the pond.

DVD (digital versatile disk; DVDs)
a circular piece of plastic used for storing and playing music and movies
We watched a great action movie on DVD last night.

How many things can you spot beginning with "e?"

E e

eagle (eagles)
a bird that hunts for its food
An eagle has sharp claws called talons.

ear (ears)
one of two parts of your body that you hear with
Amy's hair covers her ears.

early (earlier, earliest)
before the normal time
I wake up early in summer.

earn (earning, earned)
to get money for work
I earn extra allowance for washing the car.

earring (earrings)
a piece of jewelry that is worn on the ear
My mom got a pair of earrings for her birthday.

eagles

a b c d **e** f g h i j k l m n o p q r s t u v w x y z

Earth (earth)
1 the planet we live on
*Earth travels around
the Sun.*
2 soil
*A worm is moving
through the earth.*

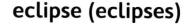
Earth

**earthquake
(earthquakes)**
a strong shaking of the earth
The earthquake did lots of damage.

Easter
a Christian holiday in March or
April
We're spending Easter at home.

easy (easier, easiest)
not difficult
This book is easy to read.

eat (eating, ate, eaten)
to take food into your mouth and
swallow it
We eat our lunch in the cafeteria.

echo (echoes)
a sound that bounces off
something and can be heard
again
Can you hear an echo?

eclipse (eclipses)
a situation where the
Moon passes in front
of the Sun and hides
it for a short time
*Next week there will be
an eclipse of the Sun.*

eel (eels)
a long fish that looks like a snake
*Eels swim thousands of miles across
the Atlantic Ocean.*

egg (eggs)
1 an oval object with a shell that
some animals lay, and from
which their babies hatch
The hen has just laid an egg.
2 an egg used as food
*Fried eggs are definitely my favorite
breakfast.*

egg

elbow (elbows)
the place where your arm bends
Ouch, I bumped my elbow.

electricity

power that is used to make lights and machines work

Lightning is a big spark of electricity.

elephant (elephants)

a large, wild animal with a long nose called a trunk

There's a new baby elephant in the zoo.

elephants

e-mail (e-mails)

a message sent by computer

I received e-mails from my friends.

e-mail (e-mailing, e-mailed)

to send a message by computer

Could you e-mail the information?

emergency (emergencies)

something very serious that happens suddenly and needs people to take action immediately

The guide told us what to do in an emergency.

empty

with nothing inside

The box is empty.

end (ends)

the place or time when something stops

Keep walking to the end of the road.

end (ending, ended)

to finish or stop

The movie ends at 6:30 p.m.

enemy (enemies)

someone who does not like you, or wants to hurt you

We are enemies, not friends.

energy

strength or power

We're trying to save energy, so we've switched off the lights.

engine (engines)

1 a machine that makes something work

Most cars have their engines at the front.

2 the part of a train that pulls the other carriages

Thomas is the name of a fictional tank engine in a series of stories.

empty

abcdefghijklmnopqrstuvwxyz

enjoy (enjoying, enjoyed)
to like to do something
I enjoy playing tennis.

enormous
very, very big
Whales are enormous creatures.

enough
as much as you need
There is enough for everyone.

enter (entering, entered)
1 to go into a place
The children entered the hall and sat down.
2 to put information into a computer
You need to enter your name and address on this form.

entrance (entrances)
the door or way in to a place
The entrance to the cave was dark.

envelope (envelopes)
a paper cover for letters and cards
Put a stamp on the envelope.

equal

environment
everything around us, such as land, air, or water
They live in a hot environment.

equal
the same as something else in number or amount
One pound is equal to 16 ounces.

equal (equaling, equaled)
to be the same as something else in number or amount
Twelve inches equal one foot.

Equator
an imaginary line around the center of the Earth
Countries near the Equator are very hot.

equipment
things that are used to do a job or activity
Our school has lots of new computer equipment.

envelopes

a b c d e f g h i j k l m n o p q r s t u v w x y z

error (errors)
a mistake
There are lots of errors in your work.

escalator (escalators)
a staircase that moves
We went up the escalator.

escape (escaping, escaped)
to get away from a place and
be free
A tiger escaped from the zoo.

**estimate (estimating,
estimated)**
to guess the size or cost of
something
We estimated the height of the tree.

evening (evenings)
the time of day between
afternoon and night time
*We don't go to school in
the evening.*

exercise

**exaggerate
(exaggerating,
exaggerated)**
to say that something is bigger or
better than it really is
*Don't exaggerate! It didn't cost
that much.*

excellent
very good
*This is an excellent book. I really
like it.*

excited
happy and interested in
something
I am excited about tomorrow.

excursion (excursions)
a trip or an outing
*We're going on an excursion to an
amusement park tomorrow.*

excuse (excuses)
a reason you give for something
that you have said or done
*Her excuse for being late is that she
couldn't find her bag.*

exercise
activity that keeps you
fit and healthy
*Don't watch television.
Go and do some exercise.*

exhibition (exhibitions)
a show where people can look at
things like paintings
*There is an exhibition of things we
made at school.*

a b c d e f g h i j k l m n o p q r s t u v w x y z

a b c d **e** f g h i j k l m n o p q r s t u v w x y z

exit (exits)
the way to leave a place
Don't use this door. The exit is over there.

expensive
costing a lot of money
Diamonds are expensive.

experiment (experiments)
a test that you do to learn something or find out if something is true
We did an experiment to see what happens when you put a magnet near a compass.

explain (explaining, explained)
to say what something means or why it has happened
Our teacher explained how the equipment worked.

explanation (explanations)
something that explains what something means or why it happened
There is a good explanation for the accident.

explode (exploding, exploded)
to suddenly burst or blow up into small pieces
The fireworks exploded in the night sky.

explore (exploring, explored)
to look around a new place
We explored the cave.

explosion (explosions)
a loud bang that you hear when something blows up
There was an explosion and then we saw a lot of smoke.

extinct
no longer existing
The dodo is an extinct bird.

extra
more than is necessary
If a lot of people come to the show, we'll need some extra chairs.

eye (eyes)
the part of the body that we use to see
I have got blue eyes.

eye

How many things can you spot beginning with "f?"

F f

face (faces)
the front part of your head
I wash my face every morning.

fact (facts)
something that is true or that really happened
We need to know all the facts.

factory (factories)
a place where things are made in large numbers by machines and people
Dad works at the car factory.

faint
1 not strong or easy to hear, see, or smell
I can't see it well because the writing is very faint.
2 feeling weak and dizzy
I feel faint because I'm very hungry.

faint (fainting, fainted)
to suddenly become weak or dizzy and fall down
It was so hot that Sophie fainted.

fair
1 good and reasonable
It's not fair that you've got more candy than me.
2 light-colored
He has fair hair.
3 fine, pleasant
The forecast says that the weather will be fair today.

fair

a b c d e **f** g h i j k l m n o p q r s t u v w x y z

a b c d e **f** g h i j k l m n o p q r s t u v w x y z

fairground (fairgrounds)
a place in the open air with rides and stalls
There are bumper cars and a roller coaster at the fairground.

fairy (fairies)
a person with magic powers in stories
There are good fairies and a bad fairy in Sleeping Beauty.

fairy

fairy tale (fairy tales)
a story for children about magical things
Cinderella is my favorite fairy tale.

fake
not real
Her coat is made of fake fur.

fall
the time of year between summer and winter
The leaves turn red in fall.

fall (falling, fell, fallen)
to drop downward
Rose fell over.

false
not true, correct, or real
He gave a false name.

family (families)
a group of people who are related to each other
There are nine people in their family.

famous
very well known
He's a famous singer.

fan (fans)
1 an object that you hold in your hand and wave, or a machine that moves the air to make it cooler
Sit in front of the fan if you're hot.
2 someone who likes a particular thing or person very much
My dad is a fan of the Knicks.

fang

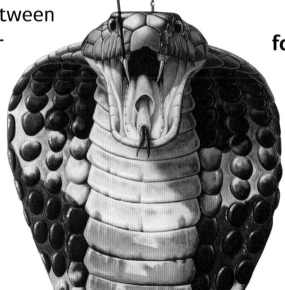

fang (fangs)
an animal's long, sharp tooth
Wolves and snakes have fangs.

far (farther, farthest; further, furthest)
not near, at a distance away
The station is near the school; it's not far.

farm (farms)
a place where people grow crops and keep animals
My uncle's farm has a lot of cows.

fast
quick, not slow
Racing cars are very fast.

fat (fatter, fattest)
weighing more than what is good or normal
It isn't healthy to be too fat.

father (fathers)
a male parent, your dad
My father was born in India.

faucet (faucets)
something that controls the flow of a liquid or gas
Turn off the faucet!

favorite
liked the best
Blue and red are my favorite colors.

fear (fearing, feared)
to be afraid that something bad is going to happen
Please don't worry; there is nothing to fear!

feast (feasts)
a large, special meal to celebrate something
Thanksgiving dinner is a feast at our house.

feather (feathers)
one of the soft, light things that cover a bird's body
The feather floated slowly to the ground.

feather

feed (feeding, fed)
to give food to a person or an animal
It's fun to feed the ducks at the pond.

father

a b c d e **f** g h i j k l m n o p q r s t u v w x y z

feel (feeling, felt)
1 to have an emotion
I feel so happy today! Dad gave me a puppy.
2 to touch something
The doctor felt my arm to see if it was broken.

female (females)
a woman, girl, or animal that can have babies when adult
The farmer separated the females from the males.

fence (fences)
a wall made of wood or wire
There is a fence between our yard and the road.

fence

ferry (ferries)
a type of ship that carries passengers over a short distance
We went to Long Island on a big ferry.

few
not many, a small number
There are only a few tickets left. Hurry up and get yours!

fiction
a story that is made up and not about real people
J. K. Rowling writes fiction for children.

fidget (fidgeting, fidgeted)
to keep moving and wriggling about
Don't fidget, please. Sit still!

field (fields)
a piece of land for growing crops, raising animals, or playing sports
There is a bull and some cows in that field.

fierce
angry and strong, or violent
Guard dogs can be very fierce.

fight (fights)
a situation where people try to hurt each other
There was a fight between two men in the parking lot.

fight (fighting, fought)
when people fight, they hit and try to hurt each other
Some people were fighting in the parking lot.

figure (figures)

1 a written number
Two hundred and fifty one in figures is 251.

2 a person's shape
She saw the figure of a woman in the shadows.

file (files)

1 a cardboard folder or a box to keep papers in
I keep my postcards in this green file.

2 information on a computer
Move your files to a new folder.

fill (filling, filled)

to put things into something until it is full
Fill the vase with water before putting the flowers in.

final (finals)

the last match in a competition
Our team is playing in the basketball final.

final

last, happening at the end
You'll find out what happens in the final chapter.

find (finding, found)

to see or get something that you are looking for
I've lost my bag. Can you help me find it?

fine

1 very thin or in small pieces
The beach is covered with fine, white sand.

2 very good
They are fine singers.

finger (fingers)

one of the five long parts on your hand
Some people wear rings on their fingers.

fingers

finish (finishing, finished)

to end
Put your pencil down when you have finished.

fire (fires)

something that burns, giving out heat and flames
We sat around the fire.

fire

a b c d e **f** g h i j k l m n o p q r s t u v w x y z

fire truck (fire trucks)
a truck used to put out fires
The fire truck went along the road flashing its lights.

firework (fireworks)
a small object that explodes into bright colors in the sky
We're going to see the fireworks in Central Park tonight.

fish (plural is the same)
a creature that lives in water
Fish have fins to help them swim, and they breathe through gills.

fist (fists)
a closed hand
Make a fist with your hand.

fish

fit (fitter, fittest)
healthy and strong
I am very fit because I walk a lot.

fit (fitting, fitted)
to be the right size
My shoes don't fit; they're too small.

fix (fixing, fixed)
1 to repair
The plumber fixed the washing machine.

fix

2 to stick or attach
Fix the picture to the wall.

fizzy (fizzier, fizziest)
having a lot of tiny bubbles
Fizzy drinks aren't very healthy.

flag (flags)
a piece of cloth that is used as a signal, or the sign of a country
The American flag has 50 stars on it.

flame (flames)
burning gas from a fire, or bright light from a candle
The candle flames lit up the room.

flash (flashes)
a burst of light
There was a flash of light in the sky.

flash (flashing, flashed)
to shine very brightly, but only for a short time
A light flashed on and off in the distance.

flashlight (flashlights)
a light that you can carry around with you
Shine the flashlight over here.

flat (flatter, flattest)
not bumpy or hilly, smooth
The ground is very flat around here.

flavors

flavor (flavors)
the taste of something
Chocolate and vanilla are flavors of ice cream.

flight (flights)
a journey in a plane
Our flight leaves at 9 o'clock.

float (floating, floated)
to lie on the water without sinking
We floated in the pool.

flood (floods)
a lot of water in a place that is usually dry
There were heavy rains and then a flood.

floor (floors)
part of a room that you stand on
There was a carpet on the floor.

Puzzle time
Can you guess these flavors?
1. v_nilla   2. choc_l_te
3. str_wberr_   4. ban_n_

Answers: 1. vanilla
2. chocolate 3. strawberry
4. banana

flour
powder made from wheat that is used to make bread and cakes
Mix the flour and butter together.

flower (flowers)
the brightly colored part of a plant that makes the seeds or fruit
Roses and daffodils are flowers.

flu (influenza)
an illness like a very bad cold
I was off school last week because I had a flu.

fly (flies)
a small insect with wings
A fly buzzed past me.

fly (flying, flew, flown)
to move through the air
Some birds fly south in winter.

fog
mist or cloud
We can't see anything because of the fog.

flying

a b c d e **f** g h i j k l m n o p q r s t u v w x y z

fold (folding, folded)
to turn or bend something over on itself
Fold your clothes neatly.

follow (following, followed)
to move after or behind someone or something
The rats followed the Pied Piper.

food **follow**
something that people or animals eat
This food tastes delicious.

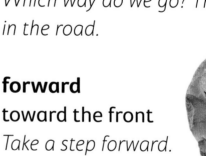

foolish
silly
It is a foolish idea.

foot (feet)
the part of your body at the end of your leg that you stand and walk on
My father has very big feet.

football
a game that is played by two teams where an oval ball is moved along the field by running with it or throwing it
I like watching football on TV.

forest (forests)
a large area of land with lots of trees growing close together
Hansel and Gretel got lost in the forest.

forget (forgetting, forgotten)
to fail to remember something
Don't forget to do your homework.

fork (forks)
1 something with a handle and points that is used for eating or digging
Use your knife and fork.
2 the place where a road or river divides in two
Which way do we go? There's a fork in the road.

forward
toward the front
Take a step forward.

fossil (fossils)
the print of an animal **fossil**
or plant that lived long ago
Fossils show us about living things millions of years ago.

fountain (fountains)
a jet of water that is pushed up
into the air
There is a fountain in the city center.

fox (foxes)
a wild animal that looks
like a dog with a bushy tail
I saw a fox in the bushes.

fox

fraction (fractions)
a part of something
*One half, one third, and
one quarter are fractions.*

frame (frames)
a wood or metal thing that fits
around a door, window, or picture
Mom put my photo in a frame.

freckle (freckles)
a small, reddish-brown spot on a
person's skin
I have freckles on my face.

free
1 not controlled, able to do what
you want
*I have free time on Wednesday
afternoon.*
2 not costing anything
It's free to get in the museum.

freeway (freeways)
a road where cars can drive fast
and travel a long way
*There aren't any stoplights or traffic
circles on a freeway.*

**freeze (freezing, froze,
  frozen)**
to turn to ice because the
temperature is very cold
Water freezes at 32°F.

fresh
1 just picked, grown, or made
Fresh fruit is healthy.
2 clean and pure
Go outside to get some fresh air.

friend (friends)
a person you know and like
My friends are coming to my party.

friendly (friendlier, friendliest)
kind and easy to get on with
We have very friendly neighbors.

**frighten (frightening,
frightened)**
to scare, to
make afraid
*Storms frighten
my dog.*

frighten

full

frog (frogs)
a creature, often green, that has long legs and lives on land and in water
There are frogs in the pond.

front
the part of something that is the most forward
I sit at the front of the class.

frost
white, icy powder that forms when it is very cold outside
The trees are covered in frost.

frown (frowning, frowned)
to have a sad, angry, or worried look on your face
What's the matter? Why are you frowning?

fruit (fruits or fruit)
part of a plant that has seeds
Apples, oranges, and grapes are all types of fruit.

fry (frying, fried)
to cook something using oil
Fry the fish until it is cooked.

full
containing as much as possible
Is the tank full yet?

fun
an enjoyable activity
We had great fun at the party.

funny (funnier, funniest)
making you laugh
The cartoon is very funny.

fur
soft, thick hair on the skin of an animal
The kitten has soft, fluffy fur.

furniture
things such as chairs, tables, beds, and desks
We have some new furniture.

future
the time after now
I wonder what life will be like in the future.

fruit

fuzzy (fuzzier, fuzziest)
1 not clear
These pictures are fuzzy.
2 curly and soft
My hair is fuzzy.

a b c d e f g h i j k l m n o p q r s t u v w x y z

How many things can you spot beginning with "g"?

G g

gallop (galloping, galloped)
to run very fast, like a horse does
The horse galloped across the field.

galloping

game (games)
an activity with rules that you play for fun
What game shall we play?

garage (garages)
1 a building to keep a car
The garage is next to the house.
2 a place where cars are repaired
The car is at the garage.

garbage
1 paper and other things that are no longer needed
Put all the garbage in the bin.
2 something that is wrong or silly
Don't talk garbage!

a b c d e f **g** h i j k l m n o p q r s t u v w x y z

abcdefghijklmnopqrstuvwxyz

gasoline
liquid fuel that makes a car engine run
We need to stop for gasoline.

gate (gates)
a door in a fence or wall
There's a gate at the end of our yard.

gentle
1 kind and careful not to hurt or disturb people or things
She is gentle with the animals.
2 not loud or strong
There is a gentle breeze.

geography
the study of the Earth, countries, and people
I like geography because we read about different people and places.

giant (giants)
an imaginary person who is very big
The story is about a giant.

gift (gifts)
something given to someone, a present
That's a lovely gift, thank you.

giraffe (giraffes)
a very tall wild animal with a long neck
Giraffes live in Africa.

girl (girls)
a female child
There are 15 girls in our class.

girls

give (giving, gave, given)
to let someone have something
We gave our teacher a present.

glad (gladder, gladdest)
happy about something
He was glad to see us.

gift

glass (glasses)
1 hard, clear material that is used to make windows, bottles, and mirrors
The bowl is made out of glass.
2 a container that you drink from
Can I please get a glass of water?

glasses
two pieces of glass or plastic that you wear to protect your eyes or to see better
I wear glasses for reading.

glitter
tiny pieces of sparkly material
We could make a birthday card and put glitter on it.

glitter (glittering, glittered)
to sparkle and shine brightly
Her necklace glittered in the sunlight.

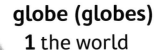
globe

globe (globes)
1 the world
He sailed around the globe.
2 a map of the world in the shape of a ball
Turn the globe around to find Australia.

gloomy (gloomier, gloomiest)
1 dark
It's a gloomy day.
2 sad
Don't look so gloomy. Smile!

glove (gloves)
a piece of clothing to wear on your hands
You need your gloves today; it's cold.

glue
a thick liquid that sticks things together
Put a dot of glue in each corner of the picture.

glue (gluing, glued)
to stick things together
I'm going to glue these pictures in my scrapbook.

Puzzle time
Which of these objects is the odd one out?
glass
jar
bottle
plate
Answer: plate

a b c d e f g h i j k l m n o p q r s t u v w x y z

a b c d e f **g** h i j k l m n o p q r s t u v w x y z

goal (goals)
1 the net and posts in a game such as hockey, where the player tries to place the ball
The goalkeeper stands in front of the goal.
2 the point given to a team when it puts the ball inside the goal
The striker scored another goal.
3 something you hope to do
My goal in life is to be a teacher.

goal

goat (goats)
a farm animal that usually has horns
Goats will eat almost anything.

gold
a valuable, yellow metal
The ring is made of gold.

goldfish (goldfish or goldfishes)
a small, orange fish that people like to keep as a pet
I feed my goldfish once a day.

good (better, best)
1 of high quality
It's a very good school.
2 pleasant
I'm having a good time.
3 well-behaved
They have been good children.

goodbye (bye)
something you say when you are leaving someone
Goodbye and good luck!

goose (geese)
a bird that looks like a big duck
There are geese on the farm.

goosebumps
bumps on your skin that appear when you are cold or frightened
I've got goosebumps!

gorilla (gorillas)
the biggest type of ape
We saw a huge gorilla at the zoo.

gorilla

grandchild (grandson, granddaughter)
the child of your children
Grandparents love seeing their grandchildren.

grandfather

grandparent (grandfather, grandmother)
the parent of your mother or father
Our grandparents live with us.

grandchildren

grape (grapes)
a small, round, juicy fruit that grows in bunches
I often eat green or purple grapes with my lunch.

grass
a green plant with thin leaves that grows over the ground
My brother is cutting the grass.

grapes

gravity
the force that pulls things toward the earth
Gravity is what makes things fall to the ground.

gravy
a brown, meaty sauce
I like gravy poured over my potatoes.

great
1 very good
This is a great song.
2 very big
There was a great storm.

greedy (greedier, greediest)
wanting or taking more food or money than is necessary
Kevin ate the whole chocolate cake. He is very greedy!

ground
1 the earth that is under your feet
Lie on the ground and look up at the stars.
2 a piece of land used for a purpose
The football ground is on the edge of town.

a b c d e f **g** h i j k l m n o p q r s t u v w x y z

a b c d e f **g** h i j k l m n o p q r s t u v w x y z

group (groups)
people or things
that are together
or connected
*The children are sitting
in groups of four.*

group

grow (growing, grew, grown)
to become bigger or longer
The flowers are growing very well.

grown-up (grown-ups)
a child's word for a man or a
woman who is no longer a child
*Some grown-ups aren't very good
at using computers.*

grumpy (grumpier, grumpiest)
in a bad mood
He's always grumpy in the morning.

guard (guards)
a person who protects something
or someone
*Four guards stood outside
the castle.*

**guard (guarding,
guarded)**
to protect something
or someone
Soldiers guard the castle.

**guess (guessing,
guessed)**
to try to give the right
answer when you are
not sure if it is correct
Guess which hand it is in.

guest (guests)
a person you invite to your house
*We've got some guests coming this
weekend.*

guinea pig (guinea pigs)
a furry animal with no tail that
people keep as a pet
We have a guinea pig.

guitar (guitars)
a stringed musical
instrument with a long neck
He plays the guitar in a band.

gun (guns)
a weapon that fires bullets
*In the movie the cowboy had a
gun.*

gym (gyms)
a place where people go to
exercise
*There are lots of different
machines at the gym.*

guitar

How many things can you spot beginning with "h?"

Hh

habit (habits)
something that you do often and do without thinking about it
Biting your nails is a bad habit.

habitat (habitats)
the place where an animal or plant lives in the wild
A frog's natural habitat is in or near a pond.

hailstones
little balls of ice that fall like rain from the sky
Hailstones that are the size of tennis balls sometimes fall in India.

hair

hair (hairs)
thin threads that grow on your skin and head
She has long, curly hair.

half

half (halves)
one of two equal parts
Would you like half an orange?

a b c d e f g **h** i j k l m n o p q r s t u v w x y z

hall (hallway; halls, hallways)
1 the room next to the main door of a house
I always take my shoes off in the hallway.
2 a big room used for meetings or parties
We do gym class in the hall.

ham
meat from a pig's leg
Would you like ham in your salad?

hamburger (hamburgers)
minced beef cooked and served in a round bun
We cooked hamburgers when we were at camp.

hammer (hammers)
a tool used for hitting nails into wood
Don't drop the hammer on your toe. It's heavy!

hammock (hammocks)
a piece of material that hangs between two poles or trees, which is used as a bed
It's fun to swing in a hammock.

hamster

hamster (hamsters)
a small, furry animal like a mouse
Hamsters keep food in their cheeks.

hand (hands)
the part of your body at the end of your arm
Your fingers and thumb are attached to your hand.

handle (handles)
the part of a bag, door, or jug that you hold on to
Hold the kettle by its handle because it is very hot.

handsome
nice-looking
Eve's neighbor is a very handsome man.

hammock

hang (hanging, hung)
to attach the top part of something, leaving the lower part free or loose
The teacher hung my picture on the wall.

hangar (hangars)
a big building where airplanes are kept
There are lots of hangars at the airport.

hanger (hangers)
a curved piece of wood or plastic to hang clothes on
Pick your shirt up and put it on a hanger.

happen (happening, happened)
to be, to take place
What a lot of noise. What's happening?

happy (happier, happiest)
feeling pleased
I'm happy because we're going on vacation tomorrow.

harbor (harbors)
a safe place for ships and boats near land
The fishing boats leave the harbor early in the morning.

hard
1 not soft
This bed is very hard.

2 difficult, not easy
The questions are very hard.

harvest (harvests)
the time of the year when farmers cut and collect crops that have been growing, or the crops themselves
The farmer had a good harvest of potatoes last year.

hat

hat (hats)
a piece of clothing that you wear on your head
You must wear a hat in the sun.

hate (hating, hated)
to strongly dislike something or someone
Our cat hates going to the veterinarian for her injections.

haunted
if a building is haunted, people think ghosts live in it
Some people say that the house on the corner is haunted.

hay
dry grass that is cut and used to feed animals
Horses and cows eat hay.

a b c d e f g **h** i j k l m n o p q r s t u v w x y z

abcdefghijklmnopqrstuvwxyz

head (heads)
1 the part of your body above your neck
Put your hands on your head.
2 a person who is the leader
The principal has her own office.

headphones
things that cover or go into the ears and through which you can listen to music without other people hearing it too
I can never hear people talking to me when I'm wearing my headphones.

healthy (healthier, healthiest)
1 well and strong
My grandad walks 3 miles every day to keep healthy.
2 good for you
Fruit and vegetables are very healthy foods.

hear (hearing, heard)
to be aware of sounds by using your ears
Can you hear a noise?

heart

heart (hearts)
1 the part of your body that pumps your blood
Your heart beats faster when you run.
2 the main part of something
The theater is in the heart of the city.
3 a shape that means love
Valentine's cards often have hearts on them.

heat (heating, heated)
to make something warm
Heat the soup but don't boil it.

heavy (heavier, heaviest)
weighing a lot
These books are heavy.

heavy

hedge (hedges)
a line of bushes along the side of a field or yard
The ball went over the hedge.

hedgehog (hedgehogs)
a small, wild animal with sharp hairs on its back
Hedgehogs curl up in a ball.

heel (heels)
1 the back part of your foot
Your heel is under your ankle.
2 the part of a shoe that is under your heel
Mom's shoes have high heels.

height
how tall something is
What is your height in inches?

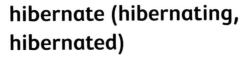

height

helicopter (helicopters)
an aircraft with blades on top that spin and make it fly
The helicopter landed in the field.

hello
what you say when you see or meet someone, or when you answer the telephone
Hello! How are you?

helmet (helmets)
a hat that protects your head
Always wear a helmet when you ride your bike.

helmet

help (helping, helped)
to make it easier for someone to do something
Let me help you carry those books.

hen (hens)
a female chicken
Hens lay eggs.

hen

here
in this place
I like it here.

hibernate (hibernating, hibernated)
to sleep during cold weather
Some animals hibernate in winter.

hide (hiding, hid, hidden)
to put yourself or something out of sight
Hide the presents, she's coming.

high
1 how long something is from the bottom to the top
How high is the mountain?
2 a long way above
The plane is high above us.

a b c d e f g **h** i j k l m n o p q r s t u v w x y z

a b c d e f g **h** i j k l m n o p q r s t u v w x y z

hill (hills)
a high piece of ground
Run down the hill.

**hippopotamus (hippo;
hippopotamuses or
hippopotami)**
a large animal that lives near
rivers and lakes in Africa
*Hippos like to
splash in
mud.*

hippo

history
things that have happened in the
past
*The history of our town is very
interesting.*

hit (hitting, hit)
to swing your hand or something
you are holding against
something else
Hit the ball as hard as you can.

hive (hives)
a box where bees live and
where they keep their honey
Thousands of bees live in each hive.

hive

hobby (hobbies)
something that you enjoy doing
in your spare time
*My hobbies are skateboarding and
listening to music.*

hockey
a game played on a field by two
teams that hit a ball using curved
wooden sticks
*We play hockey in winter and
baseball in summer.*

hold (holding, held)
to have something in your hands
or arms
Hold my coat, please.

hole (holes)
an opening or an empty space
There's a hole in the bag.

holiday (holidays)
a special day when many people
are allowed to stay away from
work or school
*Thanksgiving is a my favorite
holiday.*

hollow
empty inside
The log is hollow.

holly
a plant with shiny, prickly leaves and red berries
People use holly to make Christmas decorations.

holly

home
the place where you live
What time will you get home?

homework
school work you do at home
I need to do my math homework.

honey
a sweet, sticky food made by bees
I like honey on my oatmeal.

honey

hood (hoods)
1 a piece of clothing that covers your head, usually part of a coat
Put your hood up, it's raining.
2 the metal cover over the engine of a car
Lift the hood to look at the engine.

hoof (hooves)
the foot of an animal, such as a deer, horse, or goat
Horses have very thick hooves.

hook (hooks)
a piece of metal or plastic for hanging up or catching things
Hang your jacket on the hook.

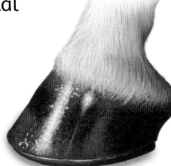
hoof

hoop (hoops)
a large ring of metal, wood, or plastic
It's fun to play with hoops.

hop (hopping, hopped)
to jump on one foot
I can hop across the room.

hope (hoping, hoped)
to wish for something
I hope you have a good time.

hop

horizon
a line in the distance where the sky appears to touch the sea
You can see a boat on the horizon.

horn (horns)
1 one of the hard, pointed things on an animal's head
Bulls have horns.
2 part of a car that makes a loud noise
The driver honked his horn.

horrible
bad or unpleasant
What a horrible color.

horse (horses)
a large animal with four legs, a mane, and a tail
My brother can ride a horse.

hospital (hospitals)
a place where sick or injured people go to get better
Have you ever stayed in hospital?

hot (hotter, hottest)
at a very high temperature
Egypt is a hot country.

hot dog (hot dogs)
a sausage in a long bun
Would you like a hot dog?

hotel (hotels)
a place people pay to stay in
We stayed in a hotel near the beach.

hour (hours)
sixty minutes
The television show lasts an hour.

house (houses)
a building that people live in
My house is at the top of the hill.

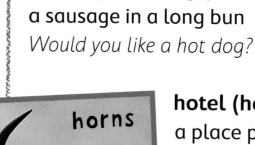
horns

house

housework
cleaning and other jobs that need to be done every day in the house
Most people hate housework.

huge
very big
There is a huge crowd waiting outside.

human (human being)
a person, not an animal
My cat is cleverer than some humans.

hump (humps)
a large bump
Some camels have two humps and others have just one.

hungry (hungrier, hungriest)
feeling that you need food
I'm hungry. What's for dinner?

hunt (hunting, hunted)
1 to look for something or someone
We hunted everywhere for the other shoe.

hurricane

2 to try to catch wild animals
Owls hunt mice at night.

hurricane (hurricanes)
a very strong wind storm
Hurricanes can cause lots of damage.

hurry (hurrying, hurried)
to do something quickly
Hurry and get your coat.

hurt (hurting, hurt)
1 to cause pain to someone
The injection won't hurt you.
2 to feel pain
My knee hurts.

husband (husbands)
the man who a woman is married to
Dad is Mom's husband.

hutch

hutch (hutches)
a box where pet rabbits live
I clean my rabbit's hutch once a day.

abcdefghijklmnopqrstuvwxyz

How many things can you spot beginning with "i?"

Ii

ice
water that is so cold that it has frozen and become hard
Let's go skating on the ice.

iceberg (icebergs)
a huge piece of ice that floats in the sea
We saw the tip of an iceberg.

iceberg

ice cream
a sweet, frozen food that is usually made from milk or cream
Ice cream tastes good on hot days.

ice hockey
a game that two teams play on ice. Players use sticks to try to hit a disk into the goal
The rubber disk used in ice hockey is called a puck.

ice cream

ice skate (ice skates)
a boot with a metal blade on the bottom for moving across ice
You can hire ice skates at the rink.

ice-skate (ice-skating, ice-skated)
to move across ice wearing ice skates
We're learning how to ice-skate.

icicle (icicles)
a thin, pointed stick of ice
There were icicles hanging from the roof.

icing
a sweet covering for cakes
Mom put chocolate icing on the cake.

icicles

idea (ideas)
a plan or a thought about how to do something
Have you any ideas about how we can raise money for the school trip?

identical
exactly the same
Tommy and Charlie are identical twins.

identical

igloo (igloos)
a house made of blocks of snow and ice
The Inuit people live in igloos in winter.

ill
not well, sick
He's feeling ill so he is going to see the doctor.

imaginary
not real
The story is about an imaginary cat with magical powers.

imagine (imagining, imagined)
to make a picture of something in your mind
Try to imagine what life was like a hundred years ago.

imitate (imitating, imitated)
to copy
The children imitated the monkeys' behavior.

immediately
now, at once, right away
Please put your clothes away immediately.

a
b
c
d
e
f
g
h
i
j
k
l
m
n
o
p
q
r
s
t
u
v
w
x
y
z

important

1 serious, useful, or valuable
It is a very important discovery.
2 powerful
The mayor is an important person in our town.

impossible

not able to be or to happen
That's impossible—you can't be in two places at once!

improve (improving, improved)
to get better
Your spelling is improving.

increase (increasing, increased)
to get bigger
The population of our town has increased a lot in the last ten years.

increase

infectious
if an illness is infectious other people can catch it easily
Measles is an infectious illness caused by a virus.

information
facts or knowledge about someone or something
There is a lot of information on our website.

impossible

initial (initials)
the first letter of a person's name
My initials are J. M.

injection (injections)
a way of putting medicine into your body using a special needle
My baby sister had an injection yesterday.

injure (injuring, injured)
to hurt yourself or someone else
The baseball player injured his leg.

ink
colored liquid that is used for writing or printing
Sign your name in ink.

innocent
an innocent person hasn't done anything wrong
He's not guilty; he's innocent.

insect (insects)
a small creature with six legs
Beetles, butterflies, and bees are all types of insect.

insects

inside
in or into a place
or container
Come inside the house; it's very cold out there.

instrument (instruments)
1 something people use to do a job
A stethoscope is an instrument that a doctor uses to listen to sounds in your body.
2 something that makes music
Guitars and violins are instruments.

instruments

Puzzle time
Can you find three insects hidden in this wordsearch?

t	r	b	e	e	o
s	d	l	e	f	w
e	u	a	y	a	a
c	a	n	d	d	s
a	e	t	r	o	p
z	x	c	t	n	o

Answers: ant bee wasp

interactive
an interactive computer program allows users to change things
In this interactive game you click on the ball to try to score a goal.

interested
wanting to pay attention to something or someone so that you can learn more
Sam is interested in sport.

interesting
exciting in a way that keeps your attention
This book is really interesting.

Internet
a huge system of linked computers all over the world that lets people communicate with each other
We use the Internet at home and at school.

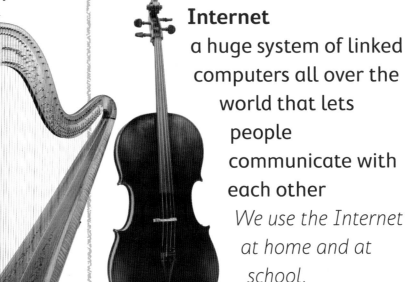

a b c d e f g h **i** j k l m n o p q r s t u v w x y z

a b c d e f g h **i** j k l m n o p q r s t u v w x y z

interrupt (interrupting, interrupted)
to stop someone who is speaking
The phone call interrupted our conversation.

invade (invading, invaded)
to attack or go into a place in large numbers
The Vikings invaded Britain in the 8th century.

invent (inventing, invented)
to make something that has not been made before
The Chinese invented paper nearly 2,000 years ago.

invention (inventions)
something new that someone makes, or produces, for the first time
The scientist is working on her new invention.

iron

investigate (investigating, investigated)
to examine something carefully to find out the truth about it
The police are still investigating the burglary.

invisible
not possible to see
You can't read it, it is written in invisible ink!

invitation (invitations)
a note or a card that asks you to go to a party
Have you replied to the party invitation?

invite (inviting, invited)
to ask someone to come somewhere with you
Ellie always invites lots of people to her parties.

iron
1 a strong, hard metal
The spade is made of iron.
2 (irons) a machine for making clothes smooth
Be careful! The iron gets very hot.

island (islands)
a piece of land that has water all around it
There's a small island in the middle of the lake.

island

How many things can you spot beginning with "j?"

J j

jacket (jackets)
a short coat
Take a jacket with you; it might be cold.

jackpot (jackpots)
the biggest prize in a lottery or competition
If I win the jackpot I'll buy you a present.

jail (jails)
a prison, a place where people are kept by the police
The thief went to jail for one year.

janitor (janitors)
a person who looks after a building
The janitor locks up the school.

jar (jars)
a glass container for storing food
Jelly and honey are sold in jars.

jars

a b c d e f g h i **j** k l m n o p q r s t u v w x y z

a
b
c
d
e
f
g
h
i
j
k
l
m
n
o
p
q
r
s
t
u
v
w
x
y
z

jealous
feeling bad because you want something that someone else has
He is jealous because I got a prize.

jeans

jeans
trousers made of denim, a strong material
My favorite clothes are jeans and a T-shirt.

jeep (jeeps)
an open vehicle that is used for driving over rough ground
I like riding in the jeep.

jelly (jellies)
a sweet food made from fruit
We had toast and jelly.

Jell-O
a clear, sweet solid food made from fruit juice
We had Jell-O and ice cream at the party.

jellyfish (jellyfish or jellyfishes)
a sea creature with a soft, clear body that may sting
I saw jellyfish at the sea life center.

jet (jets)
a fast airplane
The pop star flew to America in a private jet.

jewel (jewels)
a stone that is very valuable, such as a diamond or ruby
The crown was covered in beautiful jewels.

jewels

jewelry
necklaces, bracelets, and earrings that you wear for decoration
My mom likes to wear jewelry.

jigsaw (jigsaws)
a puzzle made from pieces that fit together to make a picture
The jigsaw has 100 pieces.

jellyfish

job (jobs)
1 work that you get paid for doing
She has a new job at the hospital.
2 something that you have to do
It's my job to take out the trash.

jockey (jockeys)
someone who rides a horse in a race
The winning jockey collected her prize.

jockey

jog (jogging, jogged)
to run slowly for exercise
My dad jogs 3 miles every morning.

join (joining, joined)
1 to become a member of a club or other group
I've joined the chess club.
2 to stick or fasten together
Join the two pieces of card with sticky tape.

joke (jokes)
a funny story that makes people laugh
Do you know any good jokes?

jolly (jollier, jolliest)
happy, always smiling
He's a jolly person.

journey (journeys)
a trip from one place to another
We were very tired after the long journey.

judge (judges)
1 the person in a court who says how to punish a guilty person
Judges often wear wigs in court.
2 a person who chooses the winner in a competition
The judges gave him nine points.

judge (judging, judged)
to say how good something is
The principal is going to judge the art competition.

Puzzle time
Look at this joke. Use the code to find out what the answer is

A	B	C	D	E	F	G	H	I	J
1	2	3	4	5	6	7	8	9	10

K	L	M	N	O	P	Q	R
11	12	13	14	15	16	17	18

S	T	U	V	W	X	Y	Z
19	20	21	22	23	24	25	26

What did one road say to the other?
13/5/5/20   25/15/21   1/20   20/8/5
3/15/18/14/5/18!

Answer: Meet you at the corner!

a b c d e f g h i **j** k l m n o p q r s t u v w x y z

a
b
c
d
e
f
g
h
i
j
k
l
m
n
o
p
q
r
s
t
u
v
w
x
y
z

judo
a Japanese fighting sport
In judo people try to throw each other to the floor.

jug (jugs)
a container with a handle for liquids
Fill the jug with water.

juice   jug

juggle (juggling, juggled)
to throw several things up in the air and catch each one quickly without dropping them
The acrobat juggled with four balls.

juice
liquid from fruit or vegetables
You can have orange juice or apple juice.

jump

jump (jumping, jumped)
to push yourself off the ground with both feet
Jump as high as you can.

jungle (jungles)
a thick forest in a hot country
The trees and plants in a jungle grow very close together.

junior
for younger people
I play the violin in the junior orchestra.

junk
things you don't want any more because they are old or no good
The garage is full of junk. Let's throw it away.

just
1 happened a very short time ago
I've only just arrived. What's happened?
2 exactly the right amount or thing
There was just enough flour to make a cake.
3 only
No, it's not a fly. It's just a bit of fluff.

How many things can you spot beginning with "k?"

Kk

kaleidoscope (kaleidoscopes)
a tube with pictures or pieces of colored glass or plastic at one end that you look through and turn to see changing patterns
The kaleidoscope was invented in 1816.

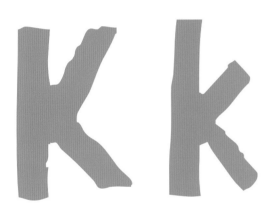

kaleidoscope

kangaroo (kangaroos)
an Australian animal that keeps its young in a pouch on the front of its body
Kangaroos have long, strong back legs.

kangaroo

karaoke
the playing of the music of songs without the words, so people can sing the words into a microphone
Karaoke started off in Japan.

karate
a Japanese fighting sport
In karate you fight using your hands and feet.

a
b
c
d
e
f
g
h
i
j
k
l
m
n
o
p
q
r
s
t
u
v
w
x
y
z

kebab (kebabs)
pieces of meat or vegetables on a stick
Let's have a takeout kebab.

keep (keeping, kept)
1 to continue to have something
You can keep the books for two weeks.
2 to continue to do something
Don't keep staring at that man.
3 to store something in a certain place
We keep the paints in the cupboard.

kennel (kennels)
a small structure, usually made out of wood, for a dog to sleep in
The man next door is making a kennel for his dog.

ketchup
a thick, cold sauce made out of tomatoes
I'd like some ketchup on my burger, please.

kick

kettle (kettles)
a container with a lid for boiling water
Come in. I'll put the kettle on and make some coffee.

key

key (keys)
1 a piece of metal used to open a lock
Have you seen my door key?
2 one of the parts of a computer or piano that you press with your fingers
Type the file name and then press the "enter" key.
3 a set of answers or an explanation of symbols
There is a key at the back of the book.

keyboard (keyboards)
the set of keys on a computer or a piano that you press to type or make a sound
This is a special keyboard with letters and pictures.

kick (kicking, kicked)
to swing your foot at something
Kick the ball into the goal!

kill (killing, killed)
to cause someone or something to die
Some weeds kill other plants.

kind
helpful, pleasant, and thoughtful
It's very kind of you to think of me.

king (kings)
a royal man who rules a country
Do you think the prince will become king?

king

kiss (kissing, kissed)
to touch someone with your lips
Mom kissed us all goodnight.

kitchen (kitchens)
the room in a house for preparing food
There are nice smells coming from the kitchen.

kite (kites)
a toy for flying in the air, made of light wood and cloth, paper, or plastic and that has a long string
Shall we fly the kite today?

kite

kitten (kittens)
a baby cat
Our cat has just had a litter of kittens.

kiwi fruit (kiwi fruits)
a green fruit with a brown, hairy skin
Mom sliced a kiwi fruit to put in the fruit salad.

kitten

knee (knees)
the part of your leg that bends
When you walk, you bend your knees.

kneel (kneeling, knelt)
to get down on your knees
Dad knelt down to stroke the cat.

knife (knives)
a tool with a blade for cutting things into pieces
Use a knife to cut the meat.

Puzzle time
How many kitchen things can you find in this word puzzle?

sinkbathovencupboardtable
chairsofashelfcupbedsaucer

Answer: 8

a b c d e f g h i j k l m n o p q r s t u v w x y z

a b c d e f g h i j **k** l m n o p q r s t u v w x y z

knight (knights)
a type of soldier who lived hundreds of years ago
Knights wore armor when they rode into battle.

knight

knit (knitting, knitted)
to make clothes or other things using wool and two long needles
Jodie knitted a scarf.

knob (knobs)
1 a round handle on a door, cupboard, or drawer
I opened the drawer and the knob came off in my hand.
2 a round switch on a radio or on a machine
Turn the knob to make it louder.

knock (knocking, knocked)
to hit something to make a noise
Someone is knocking on the door.

knot (knots)
the place where two pieces of string or rope are tied together
There's a knot in my shoelaces.

know (knowing, knew, known)
1 to have information and facts in your mind
I know that Rome is the capital of Italy.
2 to have met someone before or be familiar with them
Do you know our neighbor Mrs. White?

knuckle (knuckles)
one of the bony places in your hand where the fingers bend
When you make a fist you can see your knuckles.

koala (koalas)
an Australian animal that looks like a small gray bear
Koalas live in trees.

koala

How many things can you spot beginning with "l?"

a b c d e f g h i j k l m n o p q r s t u v w x y z

Ll

ladder (ladders)
a piece of equipment made from two long bars joined together by short bars, which you climb to reach high places
Dad uses a ladder when he paints the house.

label (labels)
a piece of paper or cloth that gives information about the thing it is attached to
Always put a label on your folders.

ladybug (ladybugs)
an insect that is red with black spots
Ladybugs are good for the yard.

ladybug

lace
fine cloth made with patterns of tiny holes
The doll's dress is made of lace.

lake

lake (lakes)
a big area of water that has land all around it
There are lots of rowing boats on the lake.

a b c d e f g h i j k **l** m n o p q r s t u v w x y z

lamb
1 (lambs) a young sheep
Lambs are born in spring.
2 meat from lambs
We had roast lamb for dinner.

lamb

lamp (lamps)
a light that you can carry around
I have a lamp on my desk.

land
1 ground
They built a house on a plot of land.
2 the dry part of Earth
The sailors were happy to see land.
3 (lands) a place or a country
The castle is in a magical land.

land (landing, landed)
to reach the ground after being in the air
The plane lands at 2:45 p.m.

language (languages)
words people use when they speak and write
French and English are languages.

lap (laps)
1 the top of your legs when you are sitting down
My cat sits on my lap.

2 once around a track
They ran 12 laps of the track.

laptop (laptops)
a small computer that you can carry around with you
Some people use laptops on trains.

large
big
We ate a large piece of cake.

laptop

larva (larvae)
a very young form of an insect
The larva of a butterfly is called a caterpillar.

laser (lasers)
a powerful light or the machine that makes it
Doctors sometimes use lasers in operations.

lasso

lasso (lassos)
a long rope with a loop at one end
The cowboy used a lasso to round up all the cattle.

last

1 after the others
We came last in the running race.
2 the most recent, the one that happened the shortest time ago
We went to Italy for our last vacation.

last (lasting, lasted)

to continue to work or to happen
How long do you think this good weather will last?

late

1 after the normal or correct time
Sorry I'm late!
2 toward the end of a period of time
It was late on Sunday afternoon when we left for town.

laugh (laughing, laughed)

to make a sound that shows you are happy, or when you think something is funny
We laughed at Dad's silly joke.

law (laws)

a rule made by the government
There are laws about children working before the age of 14.

lawn

lawn (lawns)

an area of grass that is kept short in a yard or a park
We play soccer on the lawn.

lay (laying, laid)

1 to put in a place
Lay out your colored pencils in a row.
2 to make an egg
The hens lay lots of eggs throughout the week.

lazy (lazier, laziest)

1 not wanting to work
Don't be lazy. Get up out of the armchair.
2 not busy, relaxed
We had a nice, lazy weekend at Grandma's house.

lead (leading, led)

1 to show someone the way
The guide led us through the cave's passageways.
2 to be in the front
The black horse is easily leading the race.

a b c d e f g h i j k l m n o p q r s t u v w x y z

leaf (leaves)
one of the many flat, green things on a plant or tree
Dad swept up all the leaves.

lean (leaning, leant, leaned)
1 to bend your body
Lean over to reach the ball.
2 to rest against something
Chris was leaning against the wall.

leap (leaping, leapt)
to jump into the air or over something
The fish leapt out of the water.

leap

learn (learning, learnt, learned)
to get knowledge or information about a subject
We are learning French at school.

leather
the skin of an animal that is used to make bags, shoes, and other things
My belt is made of leather.

leave (leaving, left)
1 to go away from a place
What time are you leaving?

leaf

2 to put a thing in a place or to let a thing stay in a place
You can leave your bike here.

leg (legs)
1 the part of your body between your hip and your foot that you stand on
You've got longer legs than me.
2 the part of a table or chair that holds it up
One of the chair legs is broken.

legend (legends)
a very old story about things that happened a long time ago
There are many legends about Robin Hood.

lemon (lemons)
a yellow fruit with a sour taste
I put a slice of lemon in my drink.

lemonade
a cold, sweet, fizzy drink
We drank lemonade at the party.

lend (lending, lent)
to let someone have or use something that they will return after using
Could you lend me a pen, please?

a b c d e f g h i j k **l** m n o p q r s t u v w x y z

length
how long something is
This table is 3 feet in length.

leopard (leopards)
a wild cat with yellow
fur and black spots
*Leopards are fast runners
and can climb trees.*

leopard

leotard (leotards)
a stretchy piece of clothing like a
bathing suit with sleeves
We wear leotards to do ballet.

lesson (lessons)
a time when you are learning
something from a teacher
We had two lessons in the morning.

let (letting, let)
1 to allow someone to do
something
Will your mom let you come over?
2 to allow something to happen
Just let the ball drop.

letter (letters)
1 one of the signs of the alphabet
used in writing
*There are five letters in the word
"catch."*

2 a written message that you put
in an envelope and send or give
someone
*You can either send a
letter or an e-mail.*

lettuce (lettuces)
a green, leafy vegetable
eaten in salads
We're growing lettuce this year.

library (libraries)
a place where you can borrow
books
*A mobile library comes to our
village twice a week.*

lick (licking, licked)
to put your tongue
on something
Lick your ice cream, it's going to drip.

lick

lie (lies)
something you say that you know
is not true
I told a lie and said I liked her dress.

lie (lying, lay, lain)
to have your body flat on the
floor, ground, or bed
*We put our towels on the sand and
lay down.*

lie (lying, lied)
to say something that you know
is not true
They lied about their age.

life
1 (lives) the time between when
you are born and when you die
He had a long and happy life.
2 the state of being alive
Is there is life on other planets?

lifeboat (lifeboats)
a boat that helps
people who are in
danger at sea
*The lifeboat rescued the
fishermen just in time.*

lifeboat

lift (lifting, lifted)
to move something to a higher
place
It took four people to lift our piano.

light
1 energy or brightness
from the Sun or a
lamp that lets you
see things
*Is it light enough to
take a photo?*

2 (lights) a device with a bulb
that gives out light
*Please turn off the light. It's time
for bed.*

light (lighter, lightest)
not heavy
*My bag is light because there's
nothing in it.*

lighthouse (lighthouses)
a tower on the coast that
has a bright light that
flashes to warn ships
*There's a lighthouse at the
end of the beach.*

lightning
electrical light in the sky
during a storm
*We could see lightning in the
distance.*

like (liking, liked)
1 to enjoy something or be fond
of someone or something
*I really like skateboarding
in the park.*
2 to want
*What would you like for
your birthday?*

lift

limb (limbs)
an arm or a leg
I felt dizzy and all my limbs were shaking.

line (lines)
1 a long, thin mark
Draw a line through the mistakes.
2 a piece of string, rope, or wire
Hang the clothes on the line.
3 a row
There is a line of trees at the edge of the park.

lion (lions)
a large wild cat that lives in Africa
Male lions have long hair on their heads called a mane.

lion

lip (lips)
one of the two edges of your mouth
The cat came in, licking his lips.

liquid (liquids)
something, such as water, that can be poured
Milk, juice, and water are liquids.

listen (listening, listened)
to pay attention to sound

litter

1 trash lying on the ground
We picked up all the litter.
2 (litters) the group of babies that an animal has at one time
Our dog had a litter of puppies.

little
1 small, not large
My little brother is so funny.
2 not much
We gave the cat a little milk.

live (living, lived)
1 to be alive
My uncle lived to be 90 years old.
2 to have your home in a certain place
They live in Florida now.

living room (living rooms)
a room in a house for sitting and relaxing in
The TV is in the living room.

a b c d e f g h i j k l m n o p q r s t u v w x y z

a b c d e f g h i j k **l** m n o p q r s t u v w x y z

lizard (lizards)
a small reptile with a long tail
Lizards have dry, scaly skin.

lizard

llama (llamas)
an animal from
South America
that has a soft, wooly coat
Llamas can carry heavy loads.

loaf (loaves)
bread that is baked in one piece
Get a loaf of bread from the store.

lobster (lobsters)
a sea creature with
eight legs and two claws
*We saw a lobster through
the glass-bottomed boat.*

loaf

lock (locks)
an object that closes something
that you can only open with a key
*There's a lock on my diary
to keep out my brother!*

lock

lock (locking, locked)
to close or fasten
something with a key
*Have you locked
the door?*

locker (lockers)
a narrow metal cupboard
We left our suitcase in a locker.

log (logs)
a thick piece of a tree
*It's cold. Put another log on the
fire.*

lollipop (lollipops)
a hard, round candy on a stick
I bought an orange lollipop.

lonely (lonelier, loneliest)
feeling sad that you are alone
People sometimes get lonely.

long
1 measuring a big distance
from one end to the other
We sit at a long table for lunch.
2 continuing for a large amount
of time
It's a very long movie.

look (looking, looked)
to pay attention to something
that you see
*Look at that hot-air balloon
in the sky.*

loose

1 not tight

These pants are so loose, they fall down.

loose

2 escaped, free

The bull is loose in the field. We need to catch it!

lose (losing, lost)

1 not to be able to find something

I've lost my key.

2 not to win a competition or a game

Our team lost the game by only one point.

lottery (lotteries)

a game where you can win a big prize if the numbers on your card match the winning numbers

If I win the lottery, I'll buy a fast, red car.

loud

not quiet, making a lot of noise

There was loud music coming from upstairs.

love (loving, loved)

to like someone or something very much

loud

We love our new baby.

lovely (lovelier, loveliest)

beautiful or pleasant

It's a lovely day.

low

close to the ground, not high

The Sun was low in the sky.

lucky (luckier, luckiest)

1 fortunate, having good things happen to you

They're lucky they won the lottery.

2 giving good luck

These are my lucky sneakers.

luggage

the bags and suitcases you take with you when you are traveling

I can't carry all this luggage.

lunch (lunches)

a meal that you eat in the middle of the day

What's for lunch today?

lung (lungs)

one of two parts of your body inside your chest that help you to breathe

Your two lungs are protected by bones called ribs.

a b c d e f g h i j k **l** m n o p q r s t u v w x y z

How many things can you spot beginning with "m?"

Mm

macaroni
pasta shaped like small tubes
I like macaroni with cheese sauce.

machine (machines)
a piece of equipment
that is used to
do a job
*Washing
machines
wash, rinse, and
spin your clothes.*

magnet

magazine (magazines)
a thin book with a paper cover
containing pictures and stories
*My mom buys her favorite
magazine every week.*

magic
a power to make strange things
happen
The coin disappeared by magic.

magician (magicians)
a person who does magic tricks
We had a magician at my party.

magnet (magnets)
a piece of metal that makes
some other metal objects move
toward it
A magnet will pick up all these pins.

magpie (magpies)
a big, black-and-white bird with a long tail
Magpies sometimes steal shiny objects.

magpie

mail
all the letters and packages that you send or receive in the post
He sat at his desk reading his mail.

main
the most important or the biggest
We'll meet you in front of the main entrance.

make (making, made)
1 to create or build something
I made a model of an airplane.
2 to cause something to happen or be a certain way
That joke always makes me laugh.

male (males)
a man, boy, or an animal that cannot produce eggs or have babies
The male peacock is the one with the big, colorful tail.

mammal (mammals)
a type of animal that gives birth to live babies and makes milk for them to drink
The elephant is the largest land mammal.

mammal

man (men)
an adult male
A man knocked at the door.

many (more, most)
large in number
I've been to California many times.

map (maps)
a drawing that shows where things and places are in a building, town, country, or other place
We studied a map of the world.

marble
1 a type of hard stone
The statue is made of marble.
2 (marbles) a small glass or metal ball used to play a game
I won two marbles in that last game.

marbles

a b c d e f g h i j k l **m** n o p q r s t u v w x y z

march

march (marching, marched)
to walk with regular steps
The soldiers marched in the parade.

mark (marks)
1 a sign or shape
Put a mark to show where your house is.
2 a letter or number that a teacher puts on a piece of work to show how good it is
She got good marks last semester.
3 a spot or a dark patch on something that makes it look bad
There is a mark on the carpet where we spilled the juice.

market (markets)
a place where you can buy food, clothes, plants, and other things
Most markets are outdoors.

marmalade
jelly that is made from oranges
My mom likes toast and marmalade.

marry (marrying, married)
to become husband and wife
They married three years ago.

mask (masks)
something that you put over your face to hide or protect it
She wore a mask to go to the costume party.

mast (masts)
a tall pole on a boat that holds up the sail
The pirate climbed up the mast.

mat (mats)
a piece of material, like a small carpet, that you put on the floor
Wipe your feet on the mat.

match (matches)
1 a small stick that makes a flame when you rub it against something rough
We have special long matches for lighting the fire.
2 a contest or game
That's the best tennis match I've ever seen.

match

match (matching, matched)
to go well together or be the same
Does my shirt match my pants?

mathematics (math)
the study of numbers or shapes
Mathematics is my favorite subject at school.

mattress (mattresses)
the soft, thick part of a bed that you sleep on
My mattress is too hard and I can't get to sleep.

mayonnaise
a cold, thick, creamy sauce that you put on salads
Could I have mayonnaise in my sandwich, please?

mayor (mayors)
the leader of the town or city council
The mayor came to our fall fair.

maze (mazes)
a lot of confusing paths that it is difficult to find your way through
We couldn't find our way out of the maze, but it was fun.

meadow

meadow (meadows)
a field with grass and flowers
There are lots of pretty flowers growing in the meadow.

meal (meals)
the food you eat at certain times of the day
Our main meal was roast chicken.

meal

mean
cruel or unkind
Sam and Josh, don't be mean to each other.

mean (meaning, meant)
1 to explain something or say what something is
What does the second word on the page mean?
2 to want or plan to do something
I'm very sorry, I didn't mean to hurt him.

a b c d e f g h i j k l **m** n o p q r s t u v w x y z

meaning (meanings)
the information that you get
from words and signs
*Can you explain the meaning
of this sentence?*

measles
measles
a serious illness
that that can give
you a high temperature and lots
of red spots
*When we had measles, we had to
stay in bed.*

**measure
(measuring,
measured)**
measure
to find out the
size or amount of something
We measured the line with a ruler.

meat
food that comes from the bodies
of animals
*Chicken, beef, and pork are all types
of meat.*

mechanic (mechanics)
a person who fixes cars and
machines
*My dad works as a mechanic at the
garage.*

medal (medals)
a piece of metal that is given as a
prize for winning a competition
or for doing something special
He won a medal for bravery.

medicine
1 something that you take
when you are not well so that
you will get better
*You have to take this medicine three
times a day.*
2 the study of illness and injury

*She is studying
medicine because
she wants to be a
doctor.*

medium
middle sized, between large and
small
I'd like a medium popcorn, please.

meet (meeting, met)
1 to get to know someone for the
first time
*I met my best friend Theo on the
first day of school.*
2 to go to the same place as
another person
*Let's meet at 10 o'clock in front of
the swimming pool.*

a b c d e f g h i j k l **m** n o p q r s t u v w x y z

melody (melodies)
a song or the tune of a song
The song has a strange but beautiful melody.

melon (melons)
a large fruit with a hard skin and flat seeds
Melons can be green, yellow, or orange.

melt

melt (melting, melted)
to change from a solid to a liquid when the temperature rises
The ice in my drink has melted.

memory (memories)
1 something that you remember from the past
Photographs bring back memories.
2 the ability to remember things
Do you have a good memory?
3 the part of a computer where information is stored
This computer has more memory than our old one.

mend (mending, mended)
to repair
Could you help me mend the tire?

menu (menus)
1 the list of food in a café or restaurant
The waiter brought us each a menu.
2 a list of things seen on a computer screen
Click here to go back to the main menu.

menu

mermaid (mermaids)
in stories, a sea creature with a woman's body but a fish's tail instead of legs
The mermaid was sitting on a rock combing her hair.

message (messages)
information for a person from someone else
I sent you a message by e-mail.

messy (messier, messiest)
untidy
This room is very messy.

metal
hard material such as gold, silver, copper, or iron
Coins are made out of metal.

metal

microphone

microphone (microphones)
something that is used for recording sounds or making them louder
Sing into the microphone.

microscope (microscopes)
something that makes small things look much bigger
We looked at a hair under the microscope.

microwave (microwaves)
an oven that cooks food very quickly
Heat the soup in the microwave.

midday
12:00 in the middle of the day
We'll have our lunch early—at about midday.

middle (middles)
the center or the part of something that is halfway between the beginning and the end
We sat down in the middle of the row.

midnight
12:00 in the middle of the night
We stay up until midnight on New Year's Eve.

mild
1 not too strong or serious
She had a mild case of flu.
2 not tasting too strong or too spicy
It's a mild curry.
3 not too cold, quite warm
The weather is mild today.

milk
white liquid that female mammals produce to feed their babies
I have milk on my cereal every day.

milk

mime (miming, mimed)
to act or tell a story without using any words
The children mimed scenes from the story.

mind (minds)
the part of you that helps you think and remember
I said the first thing that came into my mind.

mind (minding, minded)
1 not to like something, or to be worried by it
I don't mind what we play.
2 to be careful
Mind your head when you go through the door.
3 to look after something or someone
I'll mind your cat while you're on vacation.

mind

minus
1 the sign used in math when taking one number away from another
Twenty-five minus five equals twenty.
2 in temperature, below zero
It's cold today, it's minus one outside!

minute (minutes)
sixty seconds
We waited for twenty minutes but they didn't come.

miracle (miracles)
a wonderful thing that happens that you can't explain
It's a miracle that no one was killed in the plane crash.

mirror

mirror (mirrors)
special glass in which you can see your reflection
Go and look in the mirror; you look very pretty.

miserable
very unhappy
Don't look so miserable.

miss (missing, missed)
1 not to hit a target
He threw the ball but missed the basket.
2 to feel sad because you are not with someone
My dad is away in the army and I miss him.

mist
light fog caused by tiny drops of water forming a cloud near the ground
The mist soon cleared and the sun came out.

a b c d e f g h i j k l **m** n o p q r s t u v w x y z

mistake (mistakes)
something that is wrong
If you make a mistake, cross it out.

mitten (mittens)
a glove that does not have
separate places for each finger
Wrap up well and wear your mittens.

mix (mixing, mixed)
to put different things together
and stir them
*Mix the eggs and sugar
together.*

moat (moats)
a ditch or deep hole
around a castle
*The people in the castle
built the moat to keep
out their enemies.*

moat

model (models)
1 a small copy of something such
as a plane or a building
*We made a model of a jet plane at
the weekend.*
2 a person whose job is to show
clothes
She wants to be a model.

3 one type of something
*This computer is the most up-to-
date model.*

money
coins and paper that you use to
buy things
*Have you spent all your money
already?*

monitor (monitors)
1 the part of a
computer that shows
the screen
*It's easier to see on a
big monitor.*
2 a pupil who has a
special job to do
*I'm the book monitor
this semester.*

monkey (monkeys)
an animal with a
long tail that is
good at climbing
trees
*We watched the monkeys
at the zoo.*

monkey

monster (monsters)
a frightening creature in stories and movies
The monster chased them into the forest.

monster

month (months)
one of the twelve parts of the year
June and July are summer months.

Moon

moon (Moon; moons)
the round shining object that you see in the sky at night
The Moon goes around Earth and takes four weeks to go around once.

mop (mops)
a sponge or lots of strips of cloth on the end of a handle that you use for cleaning floors
Put the mop back in the bucket when you've finished.

more (most)
1 stronger or greater than
This book is more interesting than the one I was reading last week.

2 a bigger amount or number
Is there any more cake?

morning (mornings)
the part of the day between the time the sun comes up and noon
We get up at the same time every morning.

mosque (mosques)
a building where Muslims pray
Ali goes to the mosque every Friday.

moth (moths)
an insect that looks like a butterfly
Moths fly around at night.

mother

mother (mothers)
a woman who has a child or a female animal that has young
My mother looks after me.

motor (motors)
the part of a machine that uses power to make it work
The washing-machine motor is broken.

a b c d e f g h i j k l m n o p q r s t u v w x y z

motorbike (motorcycle; motorbikes, motorcycles)
a vehicle with two wheels and an engine
Dad has a new red-and-black motorbike.

mountain (mountains)
a very high piece of land, bigger than a hill
Some mountains have snow on top all year round.

mouse (mice)
1 a small animal with a long tail and a pointed nose
There are mice in the field, eating the corn.
2 part of a computer that you click on to move things around on the screen
You need a mouse to play this computer game.

Puzzle time
Spot five differences between these two pictures

mouse

mouth (mouths)
the part of your face with lips, teeth, and your tongue
You talk and eat using your mouth.

move (moving, moved)
to change your position or the position of something else
Can you move your head, please? I can't see.

movie (movies)
a story that is told using pictures that move
Let's watch a movie tonight.

movie theater (movie theaters)
a place you go to see movies
Shall we go to the theater?

much (more, most)
a lot
Thank you so much for coming.

mud
wet soil or earth
I'm covered in mud!

a b c d e f g h i j k l **m** n o p q r s t u v w x y z

mug (mugs)
a big cup with tall sides
Do you want a mug of hot chocolate?

mugs

multiply (multiplies, multiplying, multiplied)
to add a number to itself, often more than once
What number do you get if you multiply two by four?

music

munch (munches, munching, munched)
to eat something noisily
The rabbit munched on carrots.

muscle (muscles)
one of the parts of the body that tightens and relaxes to cause movement
My brother has got big muscles because he goes to the gym.

museum (museums)
a place where old, important, valuable, or interesting things are kept so that people can go and look at them
There is a toy museum in our town.

mushroom (mushrooms)
a small fungus with a stem and a round top that you can eat
Do you want mushrooms on your pizza?

music
a pattern of sounds that is sung or played on special instruments
The orchestra played such beautiful music.

must
to have to do something
You must put your books away.

mustache (mustaches)
the hair that grows above a man's lip
My dad has a little mustache.

mustard
a yellow or yellowish-brown sauce that tastes hot and spicy
I'd like mustard on my hot dog.

mysterious
strange, secret, or difficult to understand
He is a mysterious person; we don't know much about him.

a b c d e f g h i j k l **m** n o p q r s t u v w x y z

How many things can you spot beginning with "n?"

Nn

nail (nails)
1 a thin, sharp piece of metal with one flat end that you hit with a hammer
Hammer a nail into the wall so we can hang up the picture.
2 the hard covering on the ends of your fingers and toes
He bites his nails.

nail

name (names)
what a person or object is called
What's your name?

name

narrow
having only a short distance from one side to the other
The road is very narrow.

nasty (nastier, nastiest)
very unpleasant or bad
That's a very nasty cut.

nation (nations)
a country and the people who live there
Teams from all nations take part in the Olympic Games.

national
to do with a country or the whole country
We waved the national flag of our country.

national

nature
all the animals, plants, rivers, mountains, and other things in the world that are not made by people
I like reading books about nature.

naughty (naughtier, naughtiest)
badly behaved
Don't be naughty.

naughty

navy (navies)
the ships and people that fight for a country at sea during a war
My cousin is in the navy.

near
close by, not far
There's a bus stop near the zoo.

neat
clean or organized
His room is always neat and tidy.

necessary
if something is necessary you really need it or it must be done
It's useful to have your own computer, but it isn't necessary.

Puzzle time
Someone has been very naughty and written this message backward. Can you work out what it says?

uoy dluohs od ruoy krowemoh yreve yad

Answer: you should do your homework every day

neck (necks)
the part of your body that attaches your head to your shoulders
Put a scarf around your neck.

necklace (necklaces)
a piece of jewelry that you wear around your neck
That's a beautiful necklace.

necklace

a b c d e f g h i j k l m **n** o p q r s t u v w x y z

nectarine (nectarines)
a fruit like a peach but with a
smooth skin
This nectarine is very juicy.

need (needing, needed)
if you need something, you must
have it
*I need another notebook; this one is
full.*

needle

needle (needles)
1 a thin, sharp
piece of metal
with a hole
through it
used for sewing
*Could you thread
this needle for me, please?*
2 a thin, sharp piece of metal
through which injections are
given
The needle will not hurt you.

**neighbor
(neighbors)**
a person who
lives near you
*We invited all our
friends and
neighbors to the
party.*

nephew (nephews)
the son of your sister or brother
*My nephew is staying with us for a
few days.*

nerve (nerves)
part of your body like a long
string, which carries messages
between the brain and other
parts of the body
*There are millions of nerves in the
human body.*

nervous
worried or frightened, not able to
relax
*She's a little nervous about being in
the school play.*

nest (nests)
a place birds make to lay their
eggs
There's a robin's nest in that tree.

nest

net (nets)
material that is made
by joining pieces of
string or thread
together, leaving
spaces between them
*We use a small net
when we go fishing.*

nettle (nettles)
a wild plant with leaves that sting if you touch them
You can make tea and soup from nettles.

network (networks)
a system of things or people that are connected
This computer is part of a network.

nettle

never
not at any time, not ever
I've never been to China.

new
recently made or bought, not old
I love your jacket. Is it new?

news
information about something that is happening now or that happened a short time ago
Write soon and send us all your news.

new

newspaper (newspapers)
large sheets of paper that tell you what is happening in the world
Have you seen the front page of today's newspaper?

newspapers

next
1 the one that is nearest to you
There's an empty seat next to Jonathan.
2 the one that is immediately after someone or something else
Who's next on the list? Sarah, it's your turn.

nice
enjoyable, good, pleasant
Did you have a nice time at Grandma's house?

nickname (nicknames)
a name that your friends and family call you
My brother Rory's nickname is Rozza.

a b c d e f g h i j k l m **n** o p q r s t u v w x y z

a b c d e f g h i j k l m **n** o p q r s t u v w x y z

niece (nieces)
the daughter of your sister or brother
Her niece works in a bank.

night (nights)
the time between sunset and sunrise, when it is dark
You can see the stars on a clear night.

nightdress (nightie; nightdresses, nighties)
a dress to sleep in
Put your nightdress on and get into bed.

nightdress

nightmare (nightmares)
a bad dream
I have nightmares about giant spiders. They are very scary!

nobody
no one, no person
There's nobody home.

nonsense

nod (nodding, nodded)
to move your head up and down
You can nod your head instead of saying "yes."

noise (noises)
a loud sound
Did you hear that noise?

noisy

noisy (noisier, noisiest)
very loud or making a lot of noise
There were lots of noisy people on the beach.

none
not any, not one
I wanted some bread but there was none left.

nonsense
something that does not make any sense, or mean anything
The idea that animals can drive is complete nonsense.

no one
nobody, not one person
I have no one to talk to.

noodles
long, thin strips of pasta
Do you want rice or noodles with your beef?

noon
midday, 12:00
The bell goes at noon.

noodles

normal
something that is ordinary or usual
It's normal to feel tired first thing in the morning.

nose (noses)
the part of your face that you use for breathing and smelling things
Breathe in deeply through your nose.

nostril (nostrils)
one of the two openings at the bottom of your nose
The horse wrinkled its nostrils and tossed its head back.

note (notes)
1 a short written message
Mom wrote a note to the school.
2 a musical sound or the mark to show a musical sound
She played three notes on the piano.

nothing
not anything, zero
There's nothing in the box; it's empty.

notice (notices)
a sign that tells people something
The notice says that the play starts tomorrow.

notice (noticing, noticed)
to see something, or be aware that it is there
Did you notice if anyone was in the store?

novel (novels)
a book that tells a long story
Her latest novel is about a family in India.

nose

a b c d e f g h i j k l m **n** o p q r s t u v w x y z

now
this time, the present
My dad used to work in a factory, but he works at home now.

nowhere
not anywhere
There's nowhere else to go.

number (numbers)
1 a word or symbol that you use when you count things
Some people think seven is a lucky number.

2 the group of numbers you press when you phone someone
What's your cell number?

nurse (nurses)
a person whose job is to look after people who are sick or hurt
The nurse put a bandage on my finger.

Puzzle time
What are the missing words in these nursery rhymes?

1. Jack and Jill went up the – – – –
2. Humpty – – – – – – sat on a wall
3. Mary, Mary, quite – – – – – – – –

Answers: 1. hill 2. Dumpty 3. contrary

numbers

nursery school (nursery schools)
1 a place where young children are looked after while their parents are at work
My brother goes to nursery school.

2 a place where people grow and sell plants
My dad bought strawberry plants at the nursery.

nursery rhyme (nursery rhymes)
a poem or song for young children
My favorite nursery rhyme is Humpty Dumpty.

nut (nuts)
a seed that you can eat
Peanuts, cashews, and almonds are all different types of nut.

nuts

How many things can you spot beginning with "o?"

a b c d e f g h i j k l m n **o** p q r s t u v w x y z

oasis (oases)
an area in the desert where there is water and where trees and plants grow
There are lots of oases in the Sahara desert, but you might travel for days without seeing one.

oak (oaks)
a big tree with seeds called acorns
That oak is over two hundred years old.

oar (oars)
a pole that is wide and flat at one end and is used to row a boat
I let go of the oar and it fell into the water.

oak

ocean
1 the salt water that covers most of Earth
Strange fish live at the bottom of the ocean.
2 (oceans) a large sea
The Pacific is the largest ocean in the world.

octopus (octopuses)
a sea creature that has eight legs
The legs of an octopus are called tentacles.

octopus

off
1 away from somewhere
Take the glass off the table.
2 not in use, not switched on
Switch the computer off if you're finished with it.

office (offices)
a place where people work at desks
There are four people in my mom's office.

ogre

ogre (ogres)
a frightening giant in stories
The ogre roared until the mountains shook.

oil
1 a thick liquid made from plants or animals and used for cooking
Pour a little oil into the pan.
2 a thick liquid that comes out of the ground and is used to make gasoline
They discovered oil there last year.

3 a thick liquid that is used on metal or wood so that parts move better or more easily
This door is squeaking. Can you put some oil on it, please?

okay (OK)
1 fine, healthy, well
Are you okay?
2 all right
Is it okay if I copy my work to your computer?

old
not young, not new
We live in an old house.

once
1 one time
We've met only once before.
2 one time in a fixed period
We go swimming once a week.

onion (onions)
a vegetable that has a strong smell and taste
Peeling onions makes you cry.

online
using the Internet
I bought these sneakers online.

open

not closed or covered over

They must be at home; all the windows are open.

open (opening, opened)

1 to move a door or window so it is no longer closed

We opened the window because it was too hot.

2 to let customers in to buy things

What time does the store open?

operation (operations)

when a doctor cuts open a person's body to fix or remove something

I've got to have an operation on my eye.

open

opponent (opponents)

the person you are playing against in sport

In judo you try to throw your opponent to the ground.

opposite

1 completely different

The opposite of near is far.

2 across from, facing

They live in the house opposite ours.

orange

1 (oranges) a round, juicy fruit with a thick skin

Oranges are much sweeter than lemons.

2 the color between red and yellow

She's wearing an orange jacket.

orbit (orbiting, orbited)

to travel around and around something, like a planet in space

Earth orbits the Sun.

orchestra (orchestras)

a group of people playing musical instruments together

He plays the violin in the school orchestra.

order (ordering, ordered)

1 to ask for something in a restaurant or store

Can I order a coffee, please?

2 to tell someone what to do

The captain ordered the men to attack the ship.

ordinary
nothing special, normal
It's just an ordinary house.

ostrich (ostriches)
a large, African bird with a
long neck
Ostriches cannot fly.

ostrich

otter (otters)
a brown,
furry wild
animal that swims and eats fish
Otters feed mainly at night.

out
1 away from
The mouse got out of his cage.
2 not at home
She's out at the moment.

outdoors
not inside a building, in the open
air
It's much cooler outdoors.

oven (ovens)
something that you use to bake
or roast food
*Bake the cake in the oven for
45 minutes.*

over
1 above, on top of
We live over a cake shop.
2 finished, ended
Is the movie over yet?
3 from one side to another
She crossed over the road.

**overtake (overtaking,
overtook, overtaken)**
to go past someone or something
It's dangerous to overtake on a bend.

owl (owls)
a bird that hunts at night
*Sometimes you can
hear an owl hooting.*

**own
(owning, owned)**
to have something
that you bought or
were given
We own our house.

owl

oxygen
a gas that animals and plants
need to live
Fire needs oxygen in order to burn.

How many things can you spot beginning with "p?"

P p

paddle (paddling, paddled)
1 to move a boat through water using oars or your hands
I paddled the dinghy across the lake.

2 to walk in shallow water
My little brother can't swim yet, but he likes to paddle.

paddling

pack (packing, packed)
to put things into boxes, bags, or suitcases
Don't forget to pack your suitcases.

padlock (padlocks)
a type of lock with a metal loop that fastens things together
I chained my bike to the railings with a padlock.

package (packages)
a small parcel
This package has your name on it.

a b c d e f g h i j k l m n o **p** q r s t u v w x y z

page (pages)
one side of a sheet of paper in a book, magazine, or newspaper
This book has 384 pages.

pain (pains)
the feeling you have when you are hurt or ill
I have a bad pain in my side.

paint (paints)
a sticky liquid that you brush onto things to color them
Don't spill paint on the carpet.

paint

pair (pairs)
1 two things that go together
I need a new pair of sneakers.
2 something that is made of two similar things joined together
I've bought a new pair of sunglasses for my vacation.

palace (palaces)
a big house where a king, queen, or other important person lives
The princess lived in an old palace.

palm (palms)
1 the inside part of your hand
Fortune tellers read palms.

2 a kind of tree with leaves only at the top
Our tent was under a row of palms on the beach.

pan (pans)
a round cooking pot
Fry an egg in the pan.

pan

pancake (pancakes)
a thin, flat cake that is cooked in a frying pan
I like pancakes with sugar.

panda (pandas)
a large, black-and-white animal that is part of the bear family
Pandas come from China.

pants
a piece of clothing that covers the legs
He's wearing gray pants.

paper
1 thin sheets of material for writing or printing on
There is no paper in the printer.
2 (papers) a newspaper
My dad buys a paper every day.

parachute (parachutes)
a piece of equipment made of cloth that people wear to let them fall slowly through the air
The parachute opens automatically.

parade (parade)
a lot of people walking or marching in a long line to celebrate a special occasion
There is a parade every year.

parade

parcel (parcels)
something which is wrapped up in paper and often sent in the post
My parcel arrived today.

parent (parents)
a mother or father
My parents are both dentists.

park (parks)
a piece of ground with trees and grass
Let's go to the park to play.

park (parking, parked)
to put a car or bike in a place for a time
You can park in front of the library.

parrot (parrots)
a bird with colored feathers that usually lives in hot countries
My parrot can say my name.

parrot

part (parts)
1 one of the pieces or sections that something is divided into
Would you like part of my newspaper?
2 the role of an actor in a movie or a play
Who is playing the part of the princess?

partner (partners)
a person you work or do something with
Will you be my partner for this dance?

party (parties)
a group of people who meet to enjoy themselves
I'm having a party on Saturday.

a b c d e f g h i j k l m n o **p** q r s t u v w x y z

a b c d e f g h i j k l m n o **p** q r s t u v w x y z

pass (passing, passed)
1 to go beyond or past a person, place or thing
You'll pass the bakery on your way.
2 to succeed in doing something such as a test or an examination
I hope you pass your driving test.
3 to give someone something
Could you please pass the salt?

passengers

passenger (passengers)
someone who travels in a vehicle that is driven by someone else
This coach has seats for 48 passengers.

Passover
a Jewish holiday held in spring
The family get together for Passover.

passport (passports)
a little book showing who you are that you need when you travel to another country
You have to show your passport at the airport.

past
1 on the far side of something
The bank is on this street, just past the supermarket.
2 the time before the present
In the past, e-mail didn't exist.

pasta
food made from flour, eggs, and water, cut into shapes
We had pasta with tomato-and-mushroom sauce for lunch.

pasta

paste
1 a type of glue
I made a paste of flour and water.
2 a soft, spreadable mixture
He likes fish paste on his sandwiches.

patch (patches)
1 a small piece of material to cover a hole in something
I put a patch on my jeans.

2 a small area that is different from the area around it
There are damp patches on the wall.

patient (patients)
a person who is in hospital or visiting a doctor
This parking lot is for patients only.

patient
able to wait without complaining or getting bored
Please be patient! Dinner will be ready soon.

patio (patios)
an area outside a house with paving stones instead of grass
We sometimes have our meals on the patio.

pattern (patterns)
1 lines, shapes, or colors arranged in a certain way
The dinner plate has a pattern painted on it.
2 a shape that you copy or use as a guide to make something
Mom used a pattern to make this jacket for me.

pattern

paw (paws)
the foot of an animal
Our dog has a sore paw because she has a big thorn stuck in it.

paw

pay (paying, paid)
to give someone money for something that you are buying, or because someone has done work for you
I'll pay for the theater tickets now.

peas

pea (peas)
a small, round, green seed that is eaten as a vegetable
I had fish, fries, and peas for dinner.

peace
1 no war or fighting
There has been peace between them for many years.
2 quiet, calmness
She needed a little peace and quiet.

a b c d e f g h i j k l m n o **p** q r s t u v w x y z

a b c d e f g h i j k l m n o **p** q r s t u v w x y z

peach (peaches)
a soft fruit with a large pit inside it
This is a sweet, juicy peach.

peacock

peacock (peacocks)
a male bird with long, brightly colored tail feathers that spread out like a fan
Peacocks usually have green and blue feathers.

peanut (peanuts)
a small nut with a soft, bumpy shell
You can buy salted peanuts in small packs.

pear (pears)
a fruit with green skin that grows on a tree and that is narrow at the top and wide at the bottom
We had pears with chocolate sauce for dessert.

pebble (pebbles)
a small, smooth, round stone
We threw pebbles into the ocean.

pedal (pedals)
1 part of a bicycle that you push with your feet to make the wheels go round
Can you reach the pedals?
2 part of a car that you push with your feet to make it stop and go
The middle pedal stops the car.

peel
the skin on fruit and vegetables
You can eat the peel of an apple.

peel (peeling, peeled)
to take the skin off a fruit or a vegetable
I peeled the potatoes for lunch.

peel

peg (pegs)
1 a clip for fastening clothes to a washing line
Clothes pegs are made of wood or plastic.
2 a small hook where you can hang things
I hung my coat up on a peg.

pen (pens)
an object for drawing and writing
with ink
Sign this with a black pen.

pen

pencil (pencils)
an object with a sharp
point used for drawing
and writing
*I drew the outline using a
pencil.*

pencil

penguin (penguins)
a black-and-white sea bird that
cannot fly
Penguins are brilliant at swimming.

people
human beings; men, women, and
children
*There were a lot of people in town
today.*

pepper
1 a hot powder used to flavor
food
Please pass the salt and pepper.
2 (peppers) a sweet or
hot-tasting vegetable
*Peppers can be green,
red, yellow, or orange.*

perfume (perfumes)
a liquid with a pleasant smell
that you put on your skin
What perfume are you wearing?

person (people, persons)
a human being; a man, woman,
or child
*Our geography teacher is a very
interesting person.*

pet (pets)
an animal that is kept at
someone's home
*Do you have
any pets?*

pets

petal (petals)
one of the colored parts of a
flower
*Daffodils have bright-yellow
petals.*

phone (phones)
a telephone
*Be quiet! I'm on the
phone.*

peppers

a b c d e f g h i j k l m n o **p** q r s t u v w x y z

phone (phoning, phoned)
to call someone on the telephone
Joe phoned while you were out.

photo (photograph; photos, photographs)
a picture made with a camera
We had our photos taken for our passports.

phrase (phrases)
a group of words coming together
The phrase "a piece of cake" means easy.

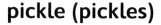
pickle

piano (pianos)
a large musical instrument with black and white keys
I play the piano.

piano

pick (picking, picked)
1 to choose
The teacher picked me for the team.
2 to break off a flower or a piece of fruit from a plant
We picked blackberries in the woods.

pickle (pickles)
vegetables in vinegar that keep fresh for a long time
I like cheese and pickle at lunchtime.

picnic (picnics)
food that you take outdoors to eat
We had a picnic in the park.

picture (pictures)
a drawing, painting, or photograph
The best picture will be in the paper.

pie (pies)
food made with fruit, vegetables, fish, or meat that is baked inside pastry
Would you like another piece of pie?

piece (pieces)
a part of something that has been separated or broken
Careful! There are some pieces of glass on the floor.

pig (pigs)
a farm animal with pink skin and a curly tail
A baby pig is called a piglet.

pig

pigeon (pigeons)
a gray bird that lives in towns
Please don't feed the pigeons!

pile (piles)
a lot of things put on top of each other
There's a pile of washing on the floor.

pile

pillow (pillows)
a cushion to put your head on in bed
I put my tooth underneath my pillow.

pilot (pilot)
the person who is in control of a plane
The pilot showed us the plane's control panel.

pilot

pin (pins)
a sharp, thin piece of metal that is used to fasten things or hold pieces of cloth together
Take all the pins out before you try the shirt on.

pin

pinch (pinching, pinched)
to squeeze between your thumb and fingers
Ow! He pinched my arm.

pineapple (pineapples)
a brown fruit that is yellow inside and has pointed leaves that stick out of the top
This slice of pineapple is very juicy.

pirate (pirates)
a person who goes onto boats and ships to steal the things they are carrying
The ship was attacked by a group of pirates.

pizza (pizzas)
a thin, flat round bread that is covered with tomatoes, cheese, and other toppings then baked in an oven
We're going to have pizza at the party.

place (places)
1 a town, area, or building
What's the name of the place where we went on vacation last year?
2 a point or position
I broke my arm in two places.

a b c d e f g h i j k l m n o **p** q r s t u v w x y z

plain

1 made of one color, having no pattern or decoration
The curtains are plain green and the carpet in plain yellow.

2 easy to understand
Can you tell me in plain English?

3 not fancy or complicated
It's a plain room, but very clean and neat.

plan (plans)

1 an idea about what will happen in the future
What are your plans for the weekend?

2 a drawing of a room, building, or other space
We drew a plan of our playground and school.

plan (planning, planned)
to think about what you want to do and how to do it
Let's plan what we're going to do this weekend.

plane (planes)
an airplane
The plane took off from the airport on time.

plane

planet (planets)
one of the very large, round objects that moves around the Sun
Venus and Mercury are planets.

plant

plant (plants)
a living thing that has roots, leaves, and seeds and can make its own food
You need to water the plants every day.

plant (planting, planted)
to put seeds or plants into the ground or containers so they will grow
Plant the flower seeds in early summer.

plaster
a thick paste that hardens when it dries
The builder spread plaster on the walls.

a b c d e f g h i j k l m n o p q r s t u v w x y z

plastic
a light material that is made from chemicals
The bucket is made of plastic.

plastic

plate (plates)
a flat dish to eat food from
Take the plates into the kitchen.

play (plays)
a story performed by actors in a theater or on the radio
I hope I get a part in the school play.

play (playing, played)
to do things that you like such as games or sports
Let's play outdoors.

playground (playgrounds)
a place for children to play
There are swings and a slide at the playground.

play

please
a word to use when you are asking for something politely
Please wait here.

plenty
enough or more than enough
There are plenty of sandwiches, so take two.

plow (plows)
a piece of equipment that farmers use to turn the soil before they plant
Modern plows can cut through the earth very quickly.

plug (plugs)
1 a piece of plastic or rubber that stops water going out of a sink or bath
Put the plug in the bath, then turn on the water.
2 a piece of plastic connected to an electrical wire that you put into a wall
Which one is the plug for the computer?

plum (plums)
a small, red, green, or purple fruit with a pit
We picked plums at the weekend.

plums

a b c d e f g h i j k l m n o **p** q r s t u v w x y z

plumber (plumbers)
a person whose job is to fix water faucets and pipes
The plumber repaired the leak.

plus
and, added to, the symbol +
Eleven plus six equals seventeen;
11 + 6 = 17.

pocket (pockets)
a small, flat bag sewn into a piece of clothing or luggage
Put your key in your pocket.

poem (poems)
writing that uses words that sound good together. The words often rhyme
This poem is very funny.

point (points)
1 a sharp end on something
Use a pencil with a sharp point.
2 a certain place or time
There's a meeting point at the airport.

Puzzle time
Can you unscramble the lines of this poem?

a. Roses red are
b. are blue Violets
c. sweet is Sugar
d. And are you so

Answer:
a. Roses are red
b. Violets are blue
c. Sugar is sweet
d. And so are you

3 the reason for something
The whole point was to raise money for the school.
4 a mark for counting a score in a game
The answer is worth one point.

point (pointing, pointed)
to use your hand or finger to show where something is
Point to where the gate is.

poison (poisons)
something that will kill you or make you very ill if you swallow it
In the movie the cook put poison in the soup.

poisonous

poisonous
harmful, containing poison
Some wild mushrooms are poisonous.

polar bear (polar bears)
a large, white bear that lives near the North Pole
Polar bears hunt fish and seals.

polar bear

pole (poles)
a long narrow piece of wood, plastic, or metal
We forgot to take the tent poles.

police
people whose job is to make sure everyone obeys the law
Do you think we need to call the police?

polite
speaking or acting in a pleasant and not rude way
It is polite to say please, thank you, and excuse me.

pollen
yellow or orange powder found inside flowers
Bees carry pollen from one flower to another.

pollen

pond (ponds)
a small area of water
There are fish in the pond.

pony (ponies)
a small horse
I had a ride on a pony.

pool (pools)
1 a place filled with water for swimming
I like playing in my pool when the weather is warm.
2 a puddle or another small area of water
We saw tiny fish in the pools on the beach.

poor
not having enough money
Some areas of the country are very poor.

pop
1 (pops) a sudden noise
There was a loud pop when they opened the bottle.
2 a short form of popular
They are a famous pop band.

poppy (poppies)
a wild, red flower with black seeds
The field is full of poppies.

poppy

a b c d e f g h i j k l m n o **p** q r s t u v w x y z

a b c d e f g h i j k l m n o **p** q r s t u v w x y z

popular
liked by a lot of people
Fishing is a popular hobby.

porcupine (porcupines)
a wild animal with long sharp
hairs like needles on its back
Some porcupines can climb trees.

potato

pork
meat from a pig
*We had roast pork
and apple sauce
for dinner.*

postcard (postcards)
a small piece of card with a
picture on one side. You write on
the other side.
*I sent my grandparents a
postcard.*

poster (posters)
a large picture or
notice that you
put up on the
wall
*I've got posters on my bedroom
wall.*

post office (post offices)
a place where people buy stamps
and send letters and parcels
*Can you get me some stamps at the
post office?*

potato (potatoes)
a roundish white vegetable that
grows under the ground
Let's have baked potatoes for lunch.

pour (pouring, poured)
to make a liquid move out of or
into something
Pour the milk into the jug.

powerful
1 very strong
*A powerful tornado swept through
town.*
2 able to control other people
and things that
happen
*It is one of the most
powerful countries in
the world.*

powerful

practice
something that you do again and
again to get better at something
What time is swimming practice?

practice (practicing, practiced)
to do something regularly to improve a skill
Keep practicing your serve and you'll get better.

prefer (preferring, preferred)
to like something better than another thing
I prefer apple juice to banana milkshake.

prepare (preparing, prepared)
to get ready or to make something ready
I'm preparing for the math test tomorrow.

presents

present
1 (presents) a gift, a thing that you are given without asking for it
Thank you for my birthday presents. They're great!
2 now
The story is set in the present.

president (presidents)
the leader of an organization or a country
Susan is the president of the debate club.

press (pressing, pressed)
to push something
Press the button on the machine.

pretend (pretending, pretended)
to act like something is true when it is not
She pretended to be asleep.

pretty (prettier, prettiest)
nice to look at
What pretty flowers!

price (prices)
the amount of money that something costs
The prices are high.

prince (princes)
the son or grandson of a king or queen
The prince rode through the forest.

princess (princesses)
the daughter or granddaughter of a king or queen
The princess dreamt of a faraway place.

princess

a b c d e f g h i j k l m n o **p** q r s t u v w x y z

a b c d e f g h i j k l m n o **p** q r s t u v w x y z

print (printing, printed)
1 to put letters, numbers, or pictures on paper with a machine
Print five copies of the story.
2 to write words without joining the letters
Print your name in full.

printer (printers)
1 a machine connected to a computer that makes copies on paper
The printer is out of paper.
2 a person who prints books, newspapers, leaflets, and other things
Take the poster to the printer.

prison (prisons)
a place where people are kept under guard as punishment
The thief was sent to prison.

private
only for some people, not for everyone
The beach is private; it belongs to the hotel.

prize (prizes)
something that you win in a game or competition
First prize is a gold trophy.

prize

problem (problems)
something that is wrong and needs to be corrected
We have a problem. The water pipe is leaking.

program (programs)
a show on the radio or television
My favorite program is on TV tonight.

prison

promise (promises)
something you say you will definitely do
I always keep my promises.

promise (promising, promised)
to tell someone that you will definitely do something
Daniel promised his dad that he would behave at school.

protect (protecting, protected)
to take care of someone or something and not let it be hurt or damaged
Penguins protect their chicks.

proud
feeling happy that you or someone else has done something
My parents are proud of me.

public
for everyone
Public transportation in this town is good.

puddle (puddles)
a little pool of water on the ground or floor
There are puddles after the rain.

puddle

pull (pulling, pulled)
to move something toward you or drag something behind you
The puppy pulled its blanket on the floor.

pull

pump (pumps)
a machine that pushes a liquid or gas from one place to another
Take your bicycle pump with you.

pumpkin (pumpkins)
a big, round, orange vegetable
The children made a lantern out of a pumpkin.

pumpkin

puncture (punctures)
a hole made by a sharp object
We had a puncture on the way home.

punish (punishing, punished)
to do something bad or unpleasant to someone because they have done something wrong
Don't punish him. It was an accident.

pupil (pupils)
1 a child that goes to school
The pupils wear a dark blue uniform.
2 the black circle in the middle of your eye
Your pupil gets smaller when you look at a bright light.

a b c d e f g h i j k l m n o **p** q r s t u v w x y z

puppet (puppets)
a toy that people move by putting their hand inside it or by pulling strings attached to it
Pinocchio is a puppet at the beginning of the story.

puppy (puppies)
a young dog
Puppies love to play with toys.

puppets

pure
not mixed with anything else
This is pure apple juice.

purr (purring, purred)
to make a soft, low sound like a happy cat
Our cat purrs when you stroke underneath her chin.

purse (purses)
a bag used for keeping things in
Mom keeps a hairbrush and keys in her purse.

push (pushing, pushed)
1 to move something away from you or out of the way
He pushed past everyone to get to the front of the line.

2 to press down on something such as a key or a button
To turn off the television, you need to push the red button.

put (putting, put)
to move a thing to a place
Put the bags in the corner.

pyramid (pyramids)
1 a very old stone building with triangular walls that form a point at the top
The Egyptian pyramids were built 4,000 years ago.
2 something with this shape
The green tent is shaped like a pyramid.

python (pythons)
a large snake that kills animals for food by squeezing them
Some pythons are up to 25 feet long.

python

How many things can you spot beginning with "q?"

Qq

quack (quacking, quacked)
to make the loud sound a duck makes
The ducks quacked when they saw me coming.

quarrel (quarrels)
an angry argument
The quarrel started over whose turn it was.

quarter (quarters)
1 one of four equal, or nearly equal, parts of something
Please divide the apple into quarters.
2 a coin that is worth 25 cents
The candy bar cost a quarter.

queen

queen (queens)
the royal female ruler of a country or the wife of a king
The queen lives in a palace.

a b c d e f g h i j k l m n o p **q** r s t u v w x y z

question (questions)
something that you ask
someone
*We'll try to answer all
your questions.*

**question mark
(question marks)**
a sign like this ? that
you write at the end of a
sentence
*You need a question mark at the
end of a sentence that begins with
the word "why."*

queue (queues)
a line of people
waiting
*There was a queue
at the movie theater.*

quiche (quiches)
a tart that is filled
with eggs, cheese
and vegetables,
meat, or fish
*There's bacon in this
quiche and salmon in that one.*

quick
fast, taking a short time
E-mail is quick and easy.

quilt

quiet
1 not making a noise
Please be quiet.
2 calm and still, not busy
*The lake is quiet and
peaceful at this time of day.*

quilt (quilts)
a warm cover for a bed
*Patchwork quilts are made by
sewing pieces of cloth together.*

quit (quitting, quit)
to stop doing something or to
leave a computer
program
To quit, press Ctrl + Q.

quiz (quizzes)
a game or
competition that
tests your
knowledge
*Can you answer the
quiz questions?*

quote (quoting, quoted)
to repeat the words that
someone else has said or written
*The English teacher quoted a line
from one of Shakespeare's plays to
the class.*

Puzzle time
Can you answer all the
questions in this quiz?
1. What is a baby pig called?
2. Can penguins fly?
3. Is a tomato a fruit or
a vegetable?
4. What are the spines on
a porcupine called?

Answers: 1. piglet 2. no 3. fruit
4. quills

How many things can you spot beginning with "r?"

Rr

rabbit (rabbits)
a small, furry animal with long ears
There are rabbits living in the wood.

rabbit

race (races)
1 a competition to see who can do something the fastest
The race starts in 15 minutes.

2 a group of people with similar physical features
People of all races and beliefs can live together happily.

race

race (racing, raced)
1 to take part in a race
There were ten drivers racing in the opening heats.
2 to do something very quickly
Jessica raced through the first part of the test.

a b c d e f g h i j k l m n o p q r s t u v w x y z

racket

racket (rackets)
1 a flat, hard net on the end of a stick that you use to play some sports
Hit the ball as hard as you can with the racket.

radio (radios)
a piece of equipment that receives sounds
I like to listen to the radio when I'm in the car.

raft (rafts)
a simple flat boat made of pieces of wood tied together
They crossed the river on a raft.

rail (rails)
1 a metal or wooden bar that you can hang things on
I hang my clothes on the rail in my closet.
2 one of two metal tracks that a train runs on
They put new rails along the track.

railroad (railroads)
1 a train track
The railroad runs to the coast.
2 a system of trains
A railroad is being built in the city.

rain
water that falls from clouds in the sky
Look at that heavy rain!

rain

rain (raining, rained)
when it rains, small drops of water fall from clouds in the sky
It's raining so we can't play outside.

rainbow (rainbows)
the curve of colors that you see in the sky after it rains and the sun comes out
The colors of the rainbow are red, orange, yellow, green, blue, indigo, and violet.

raise (raising, raised)
to lift or put something in a higher place
Raise your hand if you know the answer.

Ramadan
the ninth month of the Muslim year
Muslims do not eat or drink during the day in the month of Ramadan.

raspberry (raspberries)
a small, soft, red fruit
I like raspberries with ice cream.

raspberries

rat (rats)
an animal that looks like a big mouse with a long tail
There are rats in the barn.

rattle (rattles)
a toy that makes a knocking noise when you shake it
Babies like playing with rattles.

raw
not cooked
Raw vegetables make a healthy snack.

rats

read (reading, read)
to understand words printed on a page
The teacher is reading to the class.

recipe (recipes)
a set of instructions telling you how to cook something, and what you need to make it
Can I have the recipe for this cake?

record (recording, recorded)
to write down or tape information
We recorded a song on the computer.

recorder (recorders)
a small musical instrument that you blow to make music
I play the recorder in the orchestra.

recycle (recycling, recycled)
to use something again
We're recycling newspapers and magazines at school.

referee (referees)
a person who makes sure that players in a game don't break the rules
The referee blew his whistle.

a b c d e f g h i j k l m n o p q **r** s t u v w x y z

reflection (reflections)
an image, like a copy of
something, that you
see in a mirror
or in water
*The dog
saw its reflection
in the pond.*

reflection

rehearsal (rehearsals)
a time when actors or singers
practice before appearing in
front of an audience
There's a rehearsal at lunchtime.

reindeer (reindeer)
a deer with big antlers that lives
in cold countries
Reindeer live in groups called herds.

relative (relatives)
a person in your family
We have relatives staying overnight.

**remember (remembering,
remembered)**
1 to keep information about the
past in your mind
I remember our vacation last year
2 to bring back information to
your mind
I've just remembered; my dad is out.

remind (reminding, reminded)
to cause someone to remember
something
Remind me to buy sugar.

repeat (repeating, repeated)
to say or do something again
Please repeat the question

reptile (reptiles)
a cold-blooded animal
with dry, scaly skin
Lizards are reptiles.

reptile

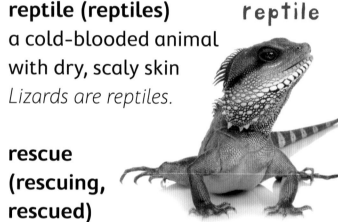

**rescue
(rescuing,
rescued)**
to save someone or something
from danger
The lifeguard rescued the children.

rest
1 a period of time when you relax
or do nothing
I'm tired. Let's have a rest.
2 the other things or people that
are left
You can have the rest of the candy.

rest (resting, rested)
to relax, to sit or lie still
I wasn't asleep; I was just resting.

restaurant (restaurants)
a place where people eat and pay for meals
A new Thai restaurant has opened.

result (results)
1 something that happens because of something else
This beautiful yard is the result of a lot of hard work.
2 a final score
Do you know the baseball results?

return (returning, returned)
1 to come back or go back to a place
He returned after the meeting.
2 to give or send something back
We returned the book to the library.

rhinoceros (rhino; rhinoceroses)
a big, wild animal with thick skin and one or two horns on its nose
There are rhinos in Africa and Asia.

rhinoceros

rhyme (rhyming, rhymed)
to end with the same sound as another word
Hat rhymes with cat.

ribbon (ribbons)
a narrow piece of material for tying up presents or decorating things
She's wearing ribbons in her hair.

rice
grains from a plant that are boiled and eaten as food
We had rice with our curry.

rice

rich
1 having a lot of money
Switzerland is a rich country.
2 food that has butter, cream, and eggs is rich food
The cheese sauce is too rich for me!

riddle (riddles)
a difficult but funny question or puzzle
I know lots of jokes and riddles.

ride (riding, rode, ridden)
to travel on a bicycle or a horse and control it as it moves
My little sister can ride a bike.

right
correct, not having any mistakes
You got all the answers right!

a b c d e f g h i j k l m n o p q **r** s t u v w x y z

a b c d e f g h i j k l m n o p q **r** s t u v w x y z

ring (rings)
1 a piece of jewelry worn on the finger
That's a pretty silver ring.
2 a circle or something that is the shape of a circle
We sat in a ring around the teacher.
3 the sound made by a bell
The phone has a loud ring.
4 a telephone call
Give me a ring tonight.

ring (ringing, rang, rung)
1 to make a sound like a bell
The doorbell rang.
2 to phone someone
Can you ring me later?

river (rivers)
a long line of water that flows to the sea
Dad is fishing by the river.

road (roads)
a track for cars, buses, and trucks to travel on
The roads are very busy today.

roar (roars)
a loud noise like the sound a lion makes
There was a roar outside the tent.

robin (robins)
a small bird with a patch of red on its front
You often see robins in winter.

robot (robots)
a machine that can do things that a person can do

robots

I wish we had a robot to do the cleaning.

rock
1 the hard, stony part of Earth's surface
We drill through rock to find oil.
2 (rocks) a large stone
We sat on the rocks by the beach.
3 a type of music that has a strong beat
My brother likes hard rock.

rocket (rockets)
1 a space vehicle shaped like a tube

rocket

The rocket is going to the Moon.
2 a firework in the shape of a tube
Rockets were exploding in the sky.

roll (rolling, rolled)
to move by turning over and over
The ball rolled from one side of the room to the other.

roofs

roof (roofs)
the covering over the top of a building or car
Rain leaked through a hole in the roof.

room (rooms)
part of a building that has its own floor, walls, and ceiling
There are four rooms upstairs in my house.

root (roots)
the part of a plant that is under the ground
Roots take water from the soil to keep the plant alive.

roots

rope (ropes)
very thick string
Tie the rope tightly so it doesn't come undone.

rose (roses)
a flower that grows on a stem with thorns
The roses bloom in summer.

rough
1 uneven, not smooth
We drove along the rough track.
2 not gentle
Don't be rough with the puppy. He's only young!

route (routes)
the way to go to a place
We took the quickest route to Grandma's house.

row (rowing, rowed)
to move a small boat through water using oars
He rowed the boat across the large lake.

royal
belonging to a queen or king
The royal coach car passed by and the queen waved at everyone.

a b c d e f g h i j k l m n o p q **r** s t u v w x y z

rubber

a strong, bouncy, or stretchy material

Car and bicycle tires are made of rubber.

rubbish

things that are no longer needed

Aaron put the rubbish in the trash bag.

ruby (rubies)

a red jewel

The queen was wearing a necklace made out of rubies and diamonds.

ruby

rude

speaking or acting in a way that is not polite

It's rude not to say "please" and "thank you."

rug (rugs)

1 a small carpet

The cat likes to sleep on the rug in front of the fire.

2 a blanket

Put the rug over your feet to keep them warm.

rule (rules)

a law or guide about how something must be done

It's wrong to break the rules at school.

ruler (rulers)

1 a long, flat piece of plastic or wood used to measure things or draw straight lines

I use a ruler in math.

2 a person who has power over a country

The country didn't have a ruler when the king died.

run (running, ran, run)

1 to move your legs faster than when you are walking

Run as fast as you can!

2 to control

Mom runs her business from home.

3 to make a piece of equipment work

Run the computer program.

run

How many things can you spot beginning with "s?"

S s

sad (sadder, saddest)
unhappy
What's happened? You look so sad.

saddle (saddles)
a seat that you sit on when you are riding a horse or a bicycle
This saddle is hard and not very comfortable.

safe (safes)
a strong box with a lock where you can keep money or jewelry
We left our money and passports in the hotel safe when we went out.

safe
not dangerous
Home is where you feel good and safe.

sail

sail (sails)
a big piece of strong material fixed to a pole on a boat, which catches the wind and makes the boat move
Let's raise the sail and go.

a b c d e f g h i j k l m n o p q r **s** t u v w x y z

a b c d e f g h i j k l m n o p q r s t u v w x y z

sail (sailing, sailed)
to travel across water in a boat or ship
We sailed to Long Island on a ferry.

sailor (sailors)
someone who works on a ship
Sailors in the navy wear dark blue uniforms.

salad (salads)
vegetables or fruit mixed together, usually eaten raw
We'll put tomatoes and cucumber in the salad.

salt
very tiny grains that come from sea water and rocks, which are put on food to make it taste good
This needs a little more salt.

same
not different or changed
Look! Our clothes are exactly the same.

same

sand
tiny pieces of crushed rock
The beach is covered in beautiful, white sand.

sandal (sandals)
one of a pair of light shoes with straps that you wear in summer
I need a new pair of sandals.

sandwich (sandwiches)
two pieces of bread with cheese, meat, or vegetables in between
We'll make some sandwiches for the picnic.

Puzzle time
Can you put these sandwich instructions in the right order?
a. Next, spread one side of each slice with butter.
b. Put the cheese on one slice of bread.
c. Now put the other slice on top.
d. First, take two slices of bread.
e. Eat your sandwich

Answer: d, a, b, c, e

sandwich

sari (saris)
a dress made from a long piece of thin cloth that Indian and South Asian women wear
She was wearing a blue sari.

saucer (saucers)
a small dish that goes under a cup
We put some milk in a saucer for the kitten.

sausage (sausages)
a mixture of meat, cereal, and spices inside a case shaped like a tube
We had sausages and chips for dinner.

scales
a machine that is used for weighing things
Weigh the ingredients on the scales.

scar (scars)
the mark left on your skin after a cut has healed
I have a scar above my left eye.

scare (scaring, scared)
to frighten
This movie will really scare you!

scarecrow (scarecrows)
an object that is made to look like a person, which is put in fields to scare off birds
We made a scarecrow out of straw.

scared
feeling afraid, frightened
Please leave a light on. I'm scared of the dark.

scarf

scarf (scarves or scarfs)
a piece of material that you wear around your neck
I'm knitting a scarf.

school (schools)
the place where children go to learn things
I started school when I was five.

science (sciences)
the study of information about the world
Biology, physics, and chemistry are all types of science.

scissors
a tool for cutting things that has two sharp blades and two handles with holes for your fingers
There's a pair of scissors in the drawer.

scarecrow

a b c d e f g h i j k l m n o p q r **s** t u v w x y z

scooter (scooters)
1 a light motorbike with small wheels
Mom goes to work on her scooter.
2 a toy with two or three wheels and a long handle. You stand on it with one foot and use the other foot to push you along.

Riding a scooter is easier than riding a bike.

scooter

score (scores)
the number of points or goals each team or player has in a game
What's the score?

score (scoring, scored)
to get points in a game
They've scored another goal!

scorpion (scorpions)
a creature with eight legs, a curved tail, and a poisonous sting
Scorpions live in warm and hot countries.

scorpion

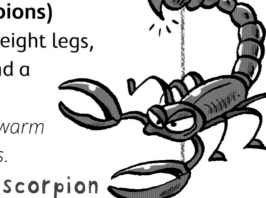

scratch (scratching, scratched)
to rub or damage your skin with your nails or something hard
Don't scratch your face.

scratch

scream (screaming, screamed)
to make a loud noise when you are afraid, angry, or hurt
The swimmers screamed when they saw the shark.

screen (screens)
a flat surface on a computer or television, or in the movie theater that has words or pictures on
You're sitting too close to the screen.

scribble (scribbling, scribbled)
to write or draw quickly and untidily
The baby's scribbled all over my homework.

sea
a large area of salty water
Look! You can see the sea from here.

seal (seals)
1 a creature that lives in the sea and eats fish
Seals are good swimmers and can dive underwater for a long time.
2 wax, plastic, or paper that you break to open a container
Do not buy this product if the seal is broken.

Seal

season (seasons)
the four parts of the year— spring, summer, fall, and winter
The weather is different in each season.

seaweed
a plant or plants that grow in or near to the sea
There was lots of seaweed floating in the water.

Seasons

secret (secrets)
something that you do not want other people to know
Please don't tell anyone else—it's a secret.

secret
if something is secret, only a few people are allowed to know about it
There's a secret passage in the house.

see (seeing, saw, seen)
1 to use your eyes to look, to watch
Did you see that show on TV last night?
2 to understand
I've explained it to you. Now do you see?
3 to meet or visit someone
We went to see Chloe in hospital.

seed (seeds)
a small part of a plant that a new plant grows from
Put the seeds in the ground.

seesaw (seesaws)
a long board that is balanced in the middle so that the ends go up and down
There's a seesaw in the playground.

a b c d e f g h i j k l m n o p q r **s** t u v w x y z

send (sending, sent)
to make something go or be
taken to another place
I sent her an e-mail yesterday.

several
some, quite a few
I've seen that movie several times.

**sew (sewing, sewed,
sewn)**
to join cloth together
with a needle and thread
I'll sew the button on for you.

shapes

shade
1 where the sun is not shining
Sit in the shade of the umbrella.
2 (shades) a thing to block out
light
*Can you pull the shade down,
please?*
3 (shades) a color
That's a nice shade of green.

shadow (shadows)
a dark shape that
appears on the ground
when something is
blocking the light
*You can see your shadow
on a sunny day.*

shake (shaking, shook, shaken)
to move something quickly up
and down or side to side
*Shake the bottle well before
opening.*

shampoo (shampoos)
liquid soap for washing your hair
Did you bring the shampoo?

shape (shapes)
the outline or
form of a thing
What shape is it?

shark (sharks)
a large fish that usually has
sharp teeth
*Some sharks can be dangerous to
humans.*

sheep (plural is the same)
a farm animal kept for wool and
meat
*There are sheep on
the hill.*

shadow

shelf (shelves)
a board, usually wooden, fixed on a wall for putting things on
Can you reach that shelf?

shell (shells)
the hard covering of an egg, a seed, or an animal such as a turtle or a crab
Ostrich eggs are very big and have thick shells.

ship (ships)
a large boat
The ship sailed across the ocean.

shirt (shirts)
a piece of clothing with buttons that you wear on the top half of your body
Tuck your shirt in.

shiver (shivering, shivered)
to shake because you are cold or scared
You're shivering! Put on your fleece.

shock (shocks)
1 a bad surprise
The check was quite a shock.

2 a pain you feel when electricity goes through your body
I got an electric shock from that socket!

shoe (shoes)
one of two coverings for your feet that are usually made of strong material
Mom's closet is full of shoes.

shoes

shoot (shooting, shot)
1 to fire a gun
Don't shoot!
2 to kick or throw a ball into a goal or net in a game
Shoot when you are closer to the basket.

short
1 not tall
My brother is too short to play basketball.
2 not long
My sister has short, brown hair.
3 not lasting a long time
Let's take a short break.

shivering

a b c d e f g h i j k l m n o p q r **s** t u v w x y z

a b c d e f g h i j k l m n o p q r s t u v w x y z

shorts
short trousers
We wear shorts in summer.

shoulder (shoulders)
the top of your arm where it joins your body
Put the bag over your shoulder.

shout (shouting, shouted)
to call out to someone in a loud voice
There's no need to shout at me; I'm right here!

shout

show (showing, showed, shown)
1 to let someone see something
Show me your new game.
2 to guide someone somewhere or help them to do something
The guide showed us around.

shower (showers)
1 something that you stand under to wash your body
Every room in the hotel has a private shower.
2 a light fall of rain
There will be showers in the afternoon.

shrink (shrinking, shrank, shrunk)
to become smaller
My favorite sweater has shrunk.

shut (shutting, shut)
to close
Shut the door, please.

sidewalk (sidewalks)
the path next to a road
Walk on the sidewalk.

sideways
toward one side, not forward or backward
Turn sideways to squeeze past.

sign (signs)
1 a mark or symbol that means something
The sign $ means dollar.
2 a notice that tells you something
The sign says "Danger!"

sign (signing, signed)
to write your name on something
Please sign your name on the form.

DANGER AVALANCHE

sign

silly (sillier, silliest)
stupid, not sensible
Don't be so silly!

similar
nearly the same as something
else
*My brother and I look similar and
we like similar things.*

**sing (singing, sang,
sung)**
to make music with
your voice
Sing us a song.

sink (sinks)
a bowl with a faucet in a kitchen
or a bathroom
Put the dirty dishes in the sink.

sink

sink (sinking, sank, sunk)
to go down below the surface
of water
*The ship Titanic sank after it
hit an iceberg.*

sister (sisters)
a girl or woman
who has the same
parents as you
Shannon is my younger sister.

sit (sitting, sat)
to put your bottom on a chair or
another type of seat
I must sit down; my feet ache.

size (sizes)
how big or small something is
These shoes come in all sizes.

skate (skates)
a boot with wheels or a blade
fixed to the bottom
*We're going to the park.
Don't forget your
skates.*

skate (skating, skated)
to move over ground or ice
wearing boots with wheels or
blades
He skated over when he saw us.

**skateboard
(skateboards)**
a small board
on wheels that you can
ride on
*He came down the
ramp on his
skateboard.*

skateboard

a b c d e f g h i j k l m n o p q r **s** t u v w x y z

skeleton (skeletons)
the bones in your body
He wore a suit with a skeleton painted on it for Halloween.

skeleton

sketch (sketching, sketched)
to draw quickly
Artists sketch a scene first.

ski (skis)
a long, flat piece of wood or plastic that you fix to special shoes for moving along on snow
We carried our skis to the top of the mountain.

ski (skiing, skied)
to move quickly over snow or water on long, narrow pieces of wood
Do you know how to ski?

skin (skins)
the outside layer covering your body, or covering fruits and vegetables
The skin is the body's largest organ.

skirt (skirts)
a piece of clothing worn by girls and women that hangs from the waist down
She was wearing a blue skirt and red jacket.

sky (skies)
the space above you where the sun, moon, stars, and clouds are
The sky was full of stars.

slap (slapping, slapped)
to hit something with an open hand
She slapped his hand.

sled (sleds)
a vehicle or toy for moving across ice or snow
We built a sled out of an old wooden box.

sleep (sleeping, slept)
not to be awake
The baby is sleeping.

sleeping

slice (slices)
a thin piece of bread, cake, meat, or other food that has been cut from a bigger piece
Can you eat another slice of meat?

slices

slide (slides)
a structure with steps and a slope that you climb then slide smoothly down
My favorite thing in the playground is the slide.

slide (sliding, slid)
to move across or down a smooth surface
The car slid across the ice and hit the tree.

slipper (slippers)
one of a pair of soft shoes that you wear indoors
Put your slippers on if your feet are cold.

slow
not fast, taking a long time
This is a slow train. We're going to be late!

small
little or young
The jeans have a small pocket for coins.

smile (smiling, smiled)
to make your mouth curve up and look happy
The photographer asked us to smile.

smoke
the cloudy gas that is made when something burns
The room filled with smoke.

smooth
not rough or bumpy
You can skate on the sidewalk; it's smooth.

smoke

snack (snacks)
a small meal that you can prepare quickly
Let's just have a snack now because we're having a big meal this evening.

snail (snails)
a small creature with a soft, wet body and a shell on its back
Snails move very slowly.

snail

a b c d e f g h i j k l m n o p q r **s** t u v w x y z

snake (snakes)

a creature with a
long body and
no legs
I hate snakes!

snake

sneaker (sneakers)

a sports shoe
I bought some new sneakers.

sneeze (sneezing, sneezed)

to blow air out of your nose
suddenly, with a loud noise
He's sneezing because he has a cold.

snow

small, soft pieces
of ice that fall
from the sky
*The trees are
covered in snow.*

snowing

**snow (snowing,
snowed)**

when it snows, small soft pieces
of ice fall from the sky
It's snowing. Let's build a snowman.

soap

something that you use with
water to wash your body
The soap is making lots of bubbles.

soccer

a game played by two teams
that try to get a round ball
between two posts
Do you like soccer?

sock (socks)

one of two pieces of clothing that
you wear on your feet
Socks keep your feet warm.

sofa (sofas)

a long, soft seat for two or more
people
Shall we sit on the sofa?

soft

1 not hard, smooth when you
touch it
The rabbit has soft fur.
2 not loud
She has a soft voice.

software

the programs that
run on a computer
He designs software.

soldier (soldiers)

a person in the army
*The soldiers marched
through the square.*

soldier

solid
hard, firm
The front door is made of solid wood.

some
1 an amount of something that is not exact
Would you like some rice?
2 part of something, but not all
Some of these apples are rotten.

son (sons)
a male child
They have two sons.

song (songs)
a piece of music with words
The children sang songs in the school hall.

Space

sore
hurting or painful
Is the cut on your leg still sore?

sorry
feeling sad because something bad or unpleasant has happened
I'm sorry your mom is ill.

soup
a liquid food made from meat or vegetables and water
Have a bowl of tomato soup.

sour
having a taste like lemons, not sweet
This juice is a bit sour.

space
1 (spaces) an empty or open place
Is there any space left in the suitcase?
2 everything beyond Earth's air
The rocket is traveling through space.

spade (spades)
a tool for digging
Turn the soil with a spade.

spaghetti
long, thin strips of pasta
Ellie likes spaghetti.

Spaghetti

spare
extra, not needed at the moment
I've got a spare pencil if you need one.

a b c d e f g h i j k l m n o p q r s t u v w x y z

speed (speeds)
how fast something moves
At what speed are we traveling?

spell (spelling, spelt, spelled)
to write or say the letters of a
word in the correct order
How do you spell "skateboard?"

Spider

spider (spiders)
a small creature
with eight legs
that catches insects in a web
There's a spider in the bathtub.

spill (spilling, spilt, spilled)
to cause a liquid to fall to the
ground accidentally
I spilt my drink on the carpet.

Spilt

Puzzle time
Can you unscramble the
names of these sports?

a. blasbeal   b. gsmwmin
c. cykeoh   d. nintes

Answers: a. baseball
b. swimming   c. hockey
d. tennis

spoon (spoons)
an object with a handle and
small bowl that is used
for eating
*We need knives,
forks, and spoons
on the table.*

Sport

sport
physical
activities such as
swimming and soccer
*Swimming is a sport the
whole family can enjoy.*

spring
the time of year
between winter and summer
The cherry tree flowers in spring.

squirrel (squirrels)
a small wild animal with a long,
bushy tail
*Squirrels are very good at climbing
trees.*

stadium (stadiums)
a big building where you can
watch sports games or concerts
*Some stadiums have roofs and some
don't.*

stairs

a set of steps in a building that go from one floor to another

I'll take the stairs to the top floor.

stamp (stamps)

1 a piece of paper that you stick on a letter or postcard before you post it

I'd like a stamp, please.

2 a tool you put ink on and then press onto something to make a mark

There's a stamp on the library book showing the date that you have to take it back.

statue

stand (standing, stood)

to be on your feet

She's standing by the door.

star (stars)

1 a ball of burning gas that looks like a light in the sky

The stars are bright tonight

2 a famous person

She's a big star now.

3 a shape with five or six points

We baked biscuits shaped like stars.

starfish (starfish or starfishes)

a star-shaped creature that lives in the ocean

There's a starfish under the rock.

start (starting, started)

to begin

We started work at 10 o'clock this morning.

station (stations)

a place where trains and buses stop to let people on and off

My dad walks to the station every morning to get the train.

statue (statues)

a model of a person or animal made out of stone or metal

There's a statue of a mermaid in the middle of the fountain.

stay (staying, stayed)

1 not to leave a place

You stay here; I'll be right back.

2 to live in a place for a short amount of time

When I was little, we stayed at my aunt's house every summer.

3 to continue to remain the same

He's never grumpy, his mood stays the same all the time.

a b c d e f g h i j k l m n o p q r **s** t u v w x y z

steal (stealing, stole, stolen)
to take something that doesn't belong to you
Thieves stole my dad's car.

steam

steam
the hot gas that comes off boiling water
The kitchen is full of steam because I forgot to put the lid on the kettle.

stick (sticks)
a long, thin piece of wood
We made a fire by rubbing two sticks together.

stomach (stomachs)
the part inside your body where food goes when you eat
My stomach hurts; I've eaten too much.

stone
1 the hard solid substance found in the ground, rock
The floor in the castle is made out of stone.
2 (stones) fourteen pounds or 6.35 kilograms
What is your weight in stones?

storm

stop (stopping, stopped)
1 to finish doing something
Stop talking for a minute.
2 not to move any more
Stop at the red light.
3 to prevent something
The referee stopped the fight.

stop lights
a set of red, orange, and green lights where two or more roads meet
Turn left at the stop lights.

store (stores)
a place that sells things
What time does the store open?

storm (storms)
very bad weather with rain, wind, and sometimes thunder and lightning
Trees fell down in the storm.

story (stories)
1 a description of events that may be real or imaginary
Do you know the story of Peter Pan?
2 the level of a building
We live on the first story.

straight
not crooked, bent, or curly
She has straight hair.

strange
1 unusual
He looks a bit strange.
2 unfamiliar
There were a lot of strange faces at the party.

stranger (strangers)
someone you don't know
You must never get into a stranger's car.

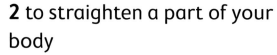
strawberries

strawberry (strawberries)
a soft, heart-shaped, red fruit
We sometimes have strawberries and cream in summer.

stream (streams)
a small river
We drank water from a mountain stream.

stretch (stretching, stretched)
1 to get longer or bigger
Pantyhose can stretch quite a bit.

2 to straighten a part of your body
She stretched her legs out under the table.

string
thick thread or thin rope
Tie some string around the box.

strong
1 powerful, not weak
She must be very strong if she can carry this suitcase.
2 not easily broken or damaged
The window is made from very strong glass.

stupid
not sensible or clever
What a stupid idea!

submarine (submarines)
a ship that can travel underwater
Submarines can help us to find out about underwater life.

submarine

sudden
happening quickly and unexpectedly
Don't make any sudden movements.

a b c d e f g h i j k l m n o p q r **s** t u v w x y z

a b c d e f g h i j k l m n o p q r **s** t u v w x y z

sugar
a sweet substance used to flavor food
Sugar can be white or brown.

suitcase (suitcases)
a case or bag to carry clothes in when you travel
Our suitcase has wheels.

summer (summers)
the time of year between spring and fall
Are you going on vacation this summer?

sun (Sun)
the very bright star that Earth travels around
All the planets in the solar system travel around the Sun.

sunflower (sunflowers)
a tall flower with a round, yellow head like the sun
Sunflowers look like big, yellow daisies.

sunflowers

sunglasses
dark glasses that you wear to protect your eyes when it is sunny
Don't forget to pack your sunglasses.

suitcases

supermarket (supermarkets)
a large store that sells food and other things
The supermarket stays open late on Fridays.

supper (suppers)
a meal you eat in the evening, or a snack you eat just before bedtime
For supper I usually have tea and toast.

surprise (surprises)
something that is completely unexpected
A bunch of flowers! What a lovely surprise!

swan (swans)
a white bird with a long neck that lives on rivers and lakes
Swans glide smoothly across the water.

sweater (sweaters)
a piece of warm clothing that covers your upper body that you pull over your head
My granny knitted me a sweater with a sun on the front.

sweep (sweeping, swept)
to brush dirt from the floor or ground
Have you swept the floor in the kitchen?

sweet
1 tasting sugary
These green grapes are very sweet.
2 kind or pleasant
That's a sweet thing to say.

swim (swimming, swam, swum)
to move through or across water by using your arms and legs
I can swim a whole length of the pool.

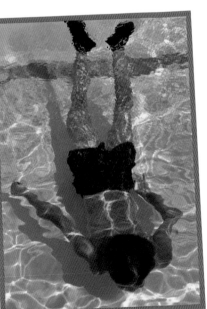

swim

sw**ord**

swimming pool (swimming pools)
a big, deep hole that contains water, where you can swim
There's an outdoor swimming pool in this town.

swing (swings)
a seat hanging from a bar or a tree that moves backward and forward
I'll sit on the swing first and you can push me.

swing (swinging, swung)
to move backward, forward, or from side to side from a fixed point
The monkey swung from tree to tree.

sword (swords)
a very large knife that was used for fighting in the past
There are lots of old swords in the museum.

synagogue (synagogues)
a building where Jewish people go to pray
My uncle got married in a synagogue.

a b c d e f g h i j k l m n o p q r **s** t u v w x y z

How many things can you spot beginning with "t?"

Tt

table (tables)
1 a piece of furniture with legs and a flat top
Please clear the table.
2 a list of numbers or words written in rows and columns
We measured the height of everyone in the class and wrote the results in a table.

tadpole (tadpoles)
a very young frog or toad
Tadpoles have big heads and long tails and live in water.

tail (tails)
the part of an animal at the end of its back
The dog has a long, white tail.

— tail

take (taking, took, taken)
1 to carry something
Take an umbrella with you.
2 to move something or someone to another place
Can you take us to the station?
3 to steal
The thieves took all the money.

talent (talents)
the ability to do something very well without having to learn it
Maya has a talent for drawing pictures of animals.

talk (talking, talked)
to speak
Simon and John talked on the phone for ages.

tall
1 higher than normal
My grandad is tall, and my grandma is short.
2 having a certain height
How tall are you?

tambourine (tambourines)
a small, round musical instrument that you shake or hit
I played the tambourine in the school concert.

tank (tanks)
1 a container for liquids
There's a leak in the gasoline tank.
2 a strong truck used by soldiers
Tanks have metal tracks or belts instead of wheels.

teacher

tape
a flat, narrow strip of plastic that is sticky on one side
Put some sticky tape on the envelope.

taste (tasting, tasted)
1 to have a flavor
What does the soup taste like?
2 to try a little food or drink to see what it is like
Have you tasted the pizza?

taxi (taxis)
a car that takes people to different places, for money
We'll take a taxi.

tea
1 a hot drink made from leaves
Do you take milk in your tea?
2 a meal you eat in the early evening
What's for tea?

teacher (teachers)
a person who gives lessons in a subject
Our teacher's name is Mr. Griffiths.

abcdefghijklmnopqrstuvwxyz

team (teams)
a group of people who play a game or work together
There are nine players in a baseball team.

tear (tears) (rhymes with ear)
a drop of water that comes out of your eye
Tears ran down his face.

tear (tearing, tore, torn) (rhymes with fair)
to rip, split, or make a hole in something
I tore the paper in half.

teddy bear (teddy bears)
a soft toy that looks like a bear
I take my teddy bear to bed with me.

telephone (telephones)
a piece of equipment that you use to speak to someone in another place
Where's your telephone?

Puzzle time
Can you match these star patterns to the names below?
1. Pegasus (the winged horse)
2. Ursa Major (Great Bear)
3. Hercules
4. Orion (the Hunter)

a

b

c

d

Answers: 1d 2b 3a 4c

telescope (telescopes)
a piece of equipment used to look at things that are far away
We looked at the stars through the telescope.

television (TV; televisions)
a machine with a screen that shows programs
What's on television tomorrow evening?

tell (telling, told)
1 to pass on information
I told you that story yesterday.
2 to know or understand
I can't tell what it means.

temple (temples)
a building where people of some religions go to pray
Hindus and Buddhists worship in a temple.

teddy bear

tennis

tennis
a game played by two or four people who hit a ball over a net to score points
Tennis is a summer game.

tent (tents)
a temporary shelter made of cloth or plastic.
The tent will keep us dry.

terrible
very bad
The movie was terrible.

tent

test (tests)
1 a set of questions to measure knowledge
We had a spelling test at school today.

2 a set of checks to find out if something is working properly
Cars must pass several tests.

text (texts)
1 a message you send by cell phone
Send me a text when you are on the train.
2 the writing in a book or magazine, not the pictures
The book has fifty pages of text.

text (texting, texted)
to send someone a message by cell phone
I'll text you later.

thank (thanking, thanked)
to tell someone you are pleased about something they have given you or have done for you
Remember to thank them for the present.

theater (theaters)
a building where you can go to see plays
Shall we go to the theater this weekend?

a b c d e f g h i j k l m n o p q r s **t** u v w x y z

thick
1 not thin
The furniture was covered with a thick sheet of plastic.
2 not watery
This pancake mixture is too thick.

thief (thieves)
a person who steals things
The police chased the thief.

thin (thinner, thinnest)
1 having not much distance from one side to the other
Cut the paper into thin strips.
2 slim, not fat
She's quite thin.
3 watery
It's a thin, clear soup.

throw

think (thinking, thought)
1 to use your mind to solve a problem or remember something
Think carefully before you answer.
2 to believe something is true, but not to know for sure
I think he likes ice cream.

thirsty (thirstier, thirstiest)
feeling that you need to drink something
Are you thirsty?

throat (throats)
the back of your mouth where food goes when you swallow
I've got a bone stuck in my throat.

through
from one side to the other
The cat came in through the cat flap.

throw (throwing, threw, thrown)
to make something go through the air
Throw the ball through the net.

thumb (thumbs)
the short, thick finger on the inside of your hand
I've cut my thumb.

thunder
the loud noise you can hear during a storm
There was thunder and lightning.

ticket (tickets)
a piece of paper that shows you have paid
I have tickets for the game on Saturday.

tickets

tidy (tidier, tidiest)
neat and organized
Leah's bedroom is never tidy.

tie (ties)
a long strip of material that you wear under a shirt collar and tie at the front
We have to wear ties in our school.

tie (tying, tied)
to join pieces of string, rope, or thread together
Tie your shoelaces.

tiger (tigers)
a large, wild cat with orange fur with black stripes
Tigers live in India and Southeast Asia.

tight
1 close-fitting
This shirt is a bit tight.
2 firmly in place
I can't undo the knot; it's too tight.

tiger

timetable (timetables)
a list of times when things happen or buses and trains leave
Check the train timetable.

tiny (tinier, tiniest)
very small
Look at the ladybug. It is so tiny!

tire (tires)
a rubber ring that goes around the wheel of a car or bicycle
I think one of the tires is flat.

tired
feeling that you need to rest
The baby is crying because it is tired.

toad (toads)
a creature like a big frog
Toads have drier skin than frogs.

toast
bread that has been cooked in a toaster or under a grill
I have toast and marmalade for breakfast.

today
this day
What's the date today?

toe (toes)
one of the five parts of your body at the end of your foot
Ouch! You stood on my toe.

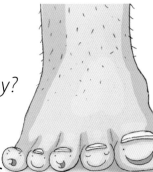

toes

together

1 joined or mixed

Mix the eggs and milk together.

2 with each other

Shall we go together?

tomatoes

tomato (tomatoes)

a red fruit that you can
eat raw or cooked

Mom sliced a tomato for the salad.

tomorrow

the day after today

What shall we do tomorrow?

tool (tools)

a piece of equipment that you use
to do a job

Hammers and saws are tools.

tongue (tongues)

the part of your body inside your
mouth that you use to speak with
and to taste things

I can curl my tongue.

tooth (teeth)

one of the hard, white
things in your mouth

*You should brush your
teeth twice a day.*

top (tops)

1 the highest part of something

*They reached the top of the
mountain.*

2 a piece of clothing for
the upper body

That's a pretty top.

3 a cover or lid for a
container

Put the top back on the bottle.

4 a toy that spins round

The top is brightly colored.

tortoise (tortoises)

a small animal with a thick, hard
shell that it can pull its legs and
head into

Tortoises move very slowly.

touch (touching, touched)

1 to put your fingers or hand on
something

Please don't touch the paintings.

2 to be so close to another thing
that there is no space between
the two

*The wires are
touching.*

teeth

towel (towels)
a cloth that you use to dry things that are wet
Dry your hands properly on the towel.

tower

tower (towers)
a tall, narrow building or part of a building
We climbed to the top of the tower.

town (towns)
a place with houses and other buildings where people live and work
There's a theater in our town.

toy (toys)
something that children like to play with
The baby has lots of toys.

toys

tractor (tractors)
a big truck that farm workers drive
We were behind a tractor on the road so we had to drive slowly.

traffic
all the cars, buses, trucks, and other vehicles that are traveling on a road
The traffic on the freeway is very heavy.

traffic circle (traffic circles)
a round place where roads meet
Turn right at the traffic circle at the end of the road.

trailer (trailers)
a small house on wheels that can be pulled behind a car
Jack and Katie have taken their trailer on vacation.

train (trains)
a line of carriages pulled by an engine on a track
Mom goes to work on the train every day.

trampoline (trampolines)
a large piece of stretchy cloth attached to a metal frame that you can bounce up and down on
We all had a go on the trampoline during gym class.

a b c d e f g h i j k l m n o p q r s **t** u v w x y z

a
b
c
d
e
f
g
h
i
j
k
l
m
n
o
p
q
r
s
t
u
v
w
x
y
z

transport (transporting, transported)
to move people or things from one place to another
The tanker transports gasoline.

trap (trapping, trapped)
to catch something in a piece of equipment
It traps mice.

trapeze (trapezes)
a bar hanging from two ropes that people swing from
I liked the acrobats on the trapeze best when we went to the circus.

travel (traveling, traveled)
to go from one place to another
They're traveling by car.

treasure
valuable things like gold or jewelry
The chest is filled with treasure.

tree (trees)
a large, tall plant with a trunk and branches
There's a big tree in our yard.

trick (tricks)
1 something clever that you do
The magician knows lots of tricks.
2 something that people do to fool or cheat someone
He played a mean trick on me.

trip (trips)
a journey
We've decided to go on a trip around the world.

trip (tripping, tripped)
to catch your foot on something and nearly fall
I tripped as I was coming down the steps.

truck (trucks)
a large vehicle for carrying things
My uncle drives a big truck.

trunk (trunks)
1 the thick part of a tree
I sat on the grass with my back against the trunk of the tree.
2 an elephant's nose
The elephant has a long trunk.
3 a box for storing things in
Where's the key for this trunk?

tree

trunk

4 a space at the back of a car where things can be stored
Put the shopping in the trunk.

try (trying, tried)
1 to make an effort
I tried to open the window.
2 to test or sample something
Have you tried this cake?

T-shirt/t-shirt (T-shirts)
a type of shirt with short sleeves and no collar
I love my purple T-shirt.

T-shirt

tunnel (tunnels)
a long hole under the ground
There is a tunnel under the sea between England and France.

turkey
1 (turkeys) a large bird that is kept on farms for its meat
There are hundreds of turkeys on the farm.
2 the meat from this bird
We usually have turkey for Thanksgiving dinner.

turn (turns)
your time to play or to do something, your go in a game
Is it my turn yet?

turn (turning, turned)
1 to move so you are looking or going in a new direction
Turn around and face the kitchen door.
2 to move something to a different position
Turn the key to open and lock the door.

turtle (turtles)
an animal that lives in water that looks like a tortoise
Turtles have thick shells covering their bodies.

twin (twins)
your brother or sister born at the same time as you
Tom and Dylan are twins.

twins

a b c d e f g h i j k l m n o p q r s t **u** v w x y z

How many things can you spot beginning with "u?"

Uu

ugly (uglier, ugliest)
not nice to look at
What an ugly color!

umbrella (umbrellas)
a piece of material stretched
over a frame with a handle, that
keeps the rain off
*It's raining
outside; I'll
take my
umbrella.*

umbrella

uncle (uncles)
the brother of your mother or
father, or the husband of your
aunt
*He looks like
his uncle.*

under
below
Put your bag   **under**
under your seat.

**understand (understanding,
understood)**
1 to know the meaning of words
or ideas
Does he understand English?
2 to know how something works
*I don't understand how the
machine works.*

3 to know how and why someone feels or acts a certain way
You don't understand.

underwear
pieces of clothing that you wear next to your body, under your other clothes
Panties and undershirts are items of underwear.

unhappy (unhappier, unhappiest)
not happy, sad
Cheer up! Try not to look so unhappy.

unicorn

unicorn (unicorns)
an animal in stories that looks like a white horse with a horn growing out of the front of its head
In the story, the prince searched for the unicorn in the forest.

uniform (uniforms)
a set of clothes worn by everyone in a group of people
In school we wear a uniform.

universe (universes)
all the planets, all the stars, the Sun, and everything in space
Is there life anywhere else in the universe?

up
toward a higher position
Pass that brush up to me.

upset
1 feeling sad or worried
She was upset to hear the bad news.
2 feeling bad or sick
He's got an upset stomach.

upside-down

upside-down
turned over so that the top is at the bottom and the bottom is at the top
Turn the bottle upside-down and the sauce will come out.

upstairs
toward or on a higher floor of a building
I went upstairs to my bedroom.

urgent
needing attention immediately
Tell the principal that it's urgent.

How many things can you spot beginning with "v?"

a b c d e f g h i j k l m n o p q r s t u **v** w x y z

V v

vanish (vanishing, vanished)
to disappear
The deer suddenly vanished.

vase (vases)
a container to put flowers in
Mom put the roses in a vase.

vacation
a time when you do not have
to work or go to school
*We're going on vacation next
week.*

vegetable (vegetables)
a plant grown for food
Carrots are my favorite vegetable.

vegetarian (vegetarians)
a person who doesn't eat meat
My best friend is a vegetarian.

van (vans)
a vehicle that is
bigger than a car
but smaller than a
truck
The plumber drove a van.

vase

vehicle (vehicles)
a machine that moves people or
things from one place to another
Cars and trucks are vehicles.

vest (vests)
a piece of clothing like a coat without sleeves that reaches the waist
Put a vest on; it's cold today.

veterinarian (veterinarians)
an animal doctor
The veterinarian is treating our dog.

view (views)
everything you can see from a place
There's a great view from this window.

village (villages)
a group of houses and buildings in the country
It's a beautiful, old village.

vinegar
a sour liquid used to keep food fresh, or to give it a sharp taste
I like vinegar on fries.

violin

violin (violins)
a musical instrument that you hold under your chin and play with a bow
My brother is learning to play the violin.

virus (viruses)
1 a very tiny living thing that can make you ill if it gets inside your body
Flu is caused by a virus.
2 a computer program that damages information stored on a computer
The virus has damaged my files.

visit (visiting, visited)
to go to see a person or a place
We visit my grandparents every Sunday.

voice (voices)
the sound you make when you are speaking or singing
I didn't recognize your voice.

volcano (volcanoes)
a mountain with an opening that sprays out lava and ash
Mount Etna in Italy is an active volcano.

volcano

vote (voting, voted)
to show which idea or person you choose by raising your hand or writing on paper
Let's vote on this idea.

a b c d e f g h i j k l m n o p q r s t u v **w** x y z

How many things can you spot beginning with "w?"

W w

waiter (waiters)
a man who serves food in a restaurant or café
The waiter gave each of us a menu.

waitress (waitresses)
a woman who serves food in a restaurant or café
Ask the waitress for the check.

waitress

wake (waking, woke, woken)
to stop sleeping
I woke up at eight o'clock.

walk (walking, walked)
to move along, putting one foot in front of the other
I walk to school every day.

walk

wall (walls)
1 the side of a room or a building
There are some pictures on the wall.
2 a structure made of stone or bricks that goes around a yard or field
We climbed over the wall.

wallet (wallets)
a folding case to keep money in
I've left my wallet at home.

wand (wands)
a special stick used by fairies, witches, and magicians to do magic
With a flick of her wand she turned the pumpkin into a coach.

w a n d

want (wanting, wanted)
if you want something, you would like to have it or do it
Do you want a sandwich?

warm
slightly hot, not cool or cold
The water is warm.

wash (washing, washed)
to clean with water
I washed my hands.

wasp (wasps)
a black-and-yellow flying insect that stings
Wasps live in nests.

w a s p

watch (watches)
a small clock that you wear on your wrist
I'd like a watch for my birthday.

watch (watching, watched)
to look at something and pay attention
We're watching the game.

water
a liquid that falls from the sky as rain
There is water in rivers and lakes.

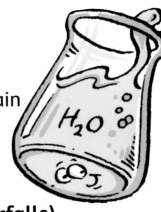

waterfall (waterfalls)
water from a stream or a river that falls straight down over rocks
There is a pool under the waterfall.

wave (waves)
1 a raised part of moving water on the sea
Waves crashed on the beach.
2 a movement of your hand from side to side to say hello or goodbye
Give them a wave.
3 the way light and sound move
Sound is carried on radio waves.

a b c d e f g h i j k l m n o p q r s t u v **w** x y z

wave (waving, waved)

1 to move your hand from side to side to say hello or goodbye
She waved to me.

2 to move from side to side
The children waved their flags.

w a v e

weak

not strong
I feel weak and dizzy.

wear (wearing, wore, worn)
to have clothes on your body
What shall I wear to the party?

weather
the condition of the air—how hot it is, the wind, rain, and clouds
What's the weather like today?

web

1 (webs) the very thin net a spider weaves
Spiders catch food in webs.

2 the World Wide Web on the Internet
You'll find the information on the web.

website (websites)
a place on the Internet where you can find out things
Please visit our website.

weed (weeds)
a plant that grows in a place where you do not want it to be
There are lots of weeds in our yard.

week (weeks)
seven days
We went to Spain for two weeks.

weekend (weekends)
Saturday and Sunday
We're going away for the weekend.

weigh (weighing, weighed)
1 to measure how heavy something is
The salesclerk weighed the fruit.

2 to be heavy or light
How much do you weigh?

w e i g h

well (wells)
a deep hole in the ground with water or oil at the bottom
People used to get water from wells.

well

1 in a good way

You played that tune very well.

2 healthy, not ill

Get well soon.

wet (wetter, wettest)

covered in water

Your hair's still wet.

whales

whale (whales)

a very large sea animal

Whales are mammals, not fish.

wheat

a cereal plant that is used to make flour

These fields are used to grow wheat.

wheel (wheels)

a round object that turns and moves a vehicle along

The wheel came off my bike.

whisker (whiskers)

one of the long, stiff hairs on an animal's face

My cat has long whiskers.

whisper (whispering, whispered)

to speak very quietly

Whisper the secret to me.

whistle (whistles)

a thing you blow into to make a loud, high sound

The referee blew his whistle.

whistle

whistle (whistling, whistled)

to blow air out through your lips and make a sound

Can you whistle?

wicked

very bad or evil

The wicked witch trapped them.

wife (wives)

the woman that a man is married to

His wife is very nice.

win (winning, won)

to be the first or the best in a race or other competition

He's won the race!

wind (winds)

air moving across the ground

There's a strong wind today.

a b c d e f g h i j k l m n o p q r s t u v **w** x y z

a b c d e f g h i j k l m n o p q r s t u v **w** x y z

windmill (windmills)

a building with long blades, called sails, that turn in the wind
Windmills were used to generate electricity.

window (windows)

an opening in a wall that is covered by glass
She looked out of the window.

wing (wings)

1 one of the parts of a bird's or insect's body that it uses for flying
The bird flapped its wings.
2 one of the flat parts of an airplane that sticks out at the side and helps the plane move through the air
I sat over the wing when I flew in a plane.

winter (winters)

the time of year between fall and spring
The weather is colder in winter.

wish (wishes)

a feeling of wanting something very much
The fairy gave me three wishes.

wish (wishing, wished)

to hope for or want something
What did you wish for?

witch (witches)

a woman in stories who has magic powers
The witch rode on a broomstick.

wizard

wizard (wizards)

a man in stories who has magic powers
The wizard broke the spell.

wolf (wolves)

a wild animal that looks like a large dog
Wolves hunt in packs, or groups.

woman (women)

a female adult
Are there any women in the team?

wolf

wonder (wondering, wondered)

to think about something and why it is that way
I wonder why she said that?

wood

1 the hard material that a tree is made of
Put more wood on the fire.

2 (woods) an area of land where a lot of trees grow
We walked through the wood.

wool

wool

thick, soft hair that grows on sheep's bodies and that can be made into thread
I need four balls of wool to knit a scarf.

work (working, worked)

1 to do a job
She works in the hospital as a doctor.

2 to go or operate smoothly
This machine is working properly now.

world

our planet and everything that is on it
There are more than six billion people in the world.

worm (worms)

a long, thin creature with no legs that lives in soil
Worms are good for the yard.

worry (worrying, worried)

to have the feeling that something bad might happen
Don't worry; I'll be all right.

worse (worst)

less good
My cold is worse today.

wrist (wrists)

the place where your arm and hand are joined
She was wearing a bracelet on her wrist.

write (writing, wrote, written)

to put words on paper using a pen or pencil
I wrote her a letter.

wrong

not right, incorrect
We've taken a wrong turn.

Puzzle time

Match the workers with the things they need to do their jobs

A	B
actor	paint
artist	theater
pilot	menu
waiter	plane

Answers: actor/theater
artist/paint pilot/plane
waiter/menu

a b c d e f g h i j k l m n o p q r s t u v **w** x y z

a b c d e f g h i j k l m n o p q r s t u v w x y z

How many things can you spot beginning with "x," "y," and "z?

xyz

X-ray (X-rays)

1 a beam of energy that can go through solid things
X-rays are used at airports.

2 a photograph of the inside of the body
The X-ray shows that his hand may be broken.

xylophone (xylophones)
a musical instrument that you play by hitting wooden or metal bars with sticks
...aby sister has a toy xylophone.

yacht (yachts)
a sailing boat
They sailed around France in a yacht.

yard (yards)
land where flowers and plants can be grown
The yard is full of flowers.

yawn (yawning, yawned)
to open your mouth and take a deep breath, usually when you are tired
You're yawning. It must be bedtime.

year (years)
a period of 12 months, especially from January to December
We've lived here for five years.

yell (yelling, yelled)
to shout very loudly
The teacher told us not to yell.

yes
a word that you say when you agree with something or when something is true
Yes, you're right.

yesterday
the day before today
I phoned you yesterday.

yoga
exercises for your body and mind
My mom does yoga on a mat.

yoghurt (or yogurt)
a thick liquid food made from milk
I'd like a strawberry yoghurt, please.

yolk (yolks)
the yellow part of an egg
I like dipping my toast into the yolk.

young
not old, not yet an adult
You're too young to walk to school on your own.

yo-yo (yo-yos)
a toy that moves up and down on a string that you hold in your hand
This yo-yo glows in the dark.

zebra

zebra (zebras)
a wild, black-and-white striped animal
Zebras look like horses.

zero
nothing, 0
The temperature is zero degrees.

zipper (zippers)
a fastener made of two rows of teeth that lock together
Some of my skirts have zippers and some have buttons.

yo-yo

zoo (zoos)
a place where wild animals are kept so that people can go to look at them
We went to the zoo on Sunday. It was great fun.

a b c d e f g h i j k l m n o p q r s t u v w x y z

ACKNOWLEDGMENTS

The publishers would like to thank the following sources for the use of their photographs:

Key t=top, b=bottom, l=left, r=right, c=center

COVER (all Shutterstock.com): Front(tc) arosoft, (b) Robert Eastman; spine(t) Vaclav Volrab; back(cl) Bjorn Heller, (bc) Eric Isselee

Dreamstime
24(b) Elena Schweitzer; 60(br) Miroslava Holasová ; 21(b) Mike Lambert

Fotolia
15 Andrew Bruce; 17 Tomasz Trojanowski; 29(r) NiDerLander; 30(b) Maksim Shebeko; 41(b); 42; 48(b) Maksim Shebeko; 58(cl); 68; 84(t) Alx; 92 Fatman73; 103(tr) Oleg Belyakov; 118(c); 134(r) Sweet Angel; 136(t) Joe Gough; 138(t) klikk; 143(b); 155(b) ivan kmit; 180(bl) Phimak; 180(cr) Eric Isselée

iStock
23(t) DNY59; 30(t) 3060917; 39 coloroftime; 48(t) janrysavy; 52 Seb Chandler; 71(b) P_Wei; 81(t) Elena Kalistratova; 89(tr) Tony Campbell; 114(b) Skeezer

Shutterstock
6 Lighthunter; 20(t) violetkaipa; 22(t) Eric Isselee; 27(b) Denis and Yulia Pogostins; 29(b) Eric Isselee; 33(b) HomeStudio; 36(t) Jose AS Reyes; 47; 62 Dudarev Mikhail; 63 Abramova Kseniya; 65(t) haveseen; 70(t) Subbotina Anna; 73(b) Andrew Buckin; 75(t) Vladimir Wrangel, (c) SiberianLena, (b) Golden Pixels LLC; 76(b) Steve Design; 78 Madlen; 79(t) Vishnevskiy Vasily, (b) Christopher Halloran; 80(t) Oleg Zhevelev, (b) loskutnikov; 82(c) terekhov igor; 83(bl) jojof, (bc) RoJo Images, (br) aabeele; 84(b) Vilainecrevette; 86(t) Valentyn Volkov, (b) michaeljung; 87(l) Kbiros, (r) Smileus; 89(br) photka; 90 Eric Isselee; 93(t) I love photo; 94(t) maxstockphoto, (c) Krasowit; 96(c) Atlaspix; 97(c) Vishnevskiy Vasily; 98(c) Sergieiev; 101(tl) Borislav Borisov; 101(bc) Mark William Penny; 105(tl) viewgene; 106(r) Yurchyks; 108(c) R.A.R. de Bruijn Holding BV; 111(t) Pavel Vakhrushev; 115(tl) marilyn barbone, (tr) ULKASTUDIO; 117(tl) infografick; 121 Vitaly Titov; 122(l) John Carnemolla, (r); 123(b) MaszaS; 124(c) Joellen Armstrong, (tr) tale; 126(t) Hurst Photo, (b) Elena Schweitzer; 127(cr) Yasonya; 128(l) Eric Isselee, (r) BestPhotoPlus; 129(b) OmniArt; 130(t) Laborant; 131(t) Sandra van der Steen, (b) Lucie Lang; 132(c) Andrew Mayovskyy; 133(t) sevenke, (c) Hurst Photo, (b) Nattika; 135(c) Mirek Srb; 137(c) Elena Schweitzer; 139(t) Stanislav Fridkin, (c) Andreas Poertner, (b) Daxiao Productions; 140(b) fivespots; 142(t) Jim Barber; 143(cr) ssuaphotos; 144(tl); 145(t) Fotokostic; 146(r) Eric Isselee; 148(t) charles taylor; 149(b) design36; 152(r) Robyn Mackenzie; 153(t) Miramiska; 157(t) Nadezda; 158(t) SergiyN, (b) Brandelet; 159(b) Tomasz Trojanowski; 161(t) Kletr, (cr) Galushko Sergey; 163(b) Aleksandra Duda; 164(b) Palto, (t); 165; 168(t) Franck Boston, (b) S-F; 176(t) Dionisvera, (b) ZouZou; 179(t) Gelpi JM; 182(b) Beata Becla; 185(b) irin-k; 186(b)

All other photographs are from: digitalSTOCK, digitalvision, Dreamstime, Fotolia, iStockphoto, John Foxx, NASA, PhotoAlto, PhotoDisc, PhotoEssentials, PhotoPro, Shutterstock, Stockbyte

All artwork from the Miles Kelly Artwork Bank

Every effort has been made to acknowledge the source and copyright holder of each picture. Miles Kelly Publishing apologizes for any unintentional errors or omissions.